"In this short book, Jen Wilkin takes the reader through the Ten Commandments with her characteristic depth, wisdom, and clarity. Whether you have studied the Bible for decades or it is brand new to you, this book will help you to understand what these ancient words mean for you today. This book makes me covet Jen Wilkin's amazing gifts of writing and teaching while giving me the tools to combat the coveting. Don't steal this book, but get it any other way you can, and you'll be glad you did."

Russell Moore, President, The Ethics & Religious Liberty Commission of the Southern Baptist Convention

"Jen Wilkin leads us to look at the Ten Commandments anew—welcoming obedience from a place of love and delight for the Lord, rather than fear and dread. For the believer set free in Christ, this is a reminder that the good news produces good fruit."

Ruth Chou Simons, *Wall Street Journal* best-selling author, *Beholding and Becoming* and *GraceLaced*; artist; Founder, GraceLaced Co.

"In *Ten Words to Live By*, Jen Wilkin does what she does best: taking Scripture and making it plain; taking theology and revealing its everyday, here-and-now practicality. And once again, we remember that God's ways and his commands are for our good. Once again, we remember that his words are life and health and peace."

Hannah Anderson, author, *All That's Good: Recovering the Lost Art of Discernment*

"Jen Wilkin has provided a fresh and timely guide through the Ten Commandments. She draws out their significance to those who follow Christ, giving us a mouth-watering vision of what life can look like as we follow the good words of King Jesus."

Sam Allberry, pastor; author, *7 Myths about Singleness* and *Why Does God Care Who I Sleep With?*

"I try to read everything Jen Wilkin writes, and this book is another example of why. I found myself informed, challenged, and encouraged, and I think you will too."

Andrew Wilson, Teaching Pastor, King's Church London

"Jen Wilkin has provided a clear, insightful, and accessible explanation of one of the most important sections of Holy Scripture—the Ten Commandments. With ease and verve she helps us understand the heart of God's laws and how they are given to bring us life. Highly recommended!"

Jonathan T. Pennington, Associate Professor of New Testament, The Southern Baptist Theological Seminary

"What I appreciate most about Jen Wilkin is that as she teaches the Bible, she also teaches us how to read the Bible for ourselves. That's exactly what she does in this book with one of the most important and yet misunderstood parts of Scripture—the Ten Commandments. Far from being cringe-worthy rules from a grumpy God, we learn that God's commands are beautiful and lifegiving, revealing the pattern of Christlikeness that we can experience by God's grace. Reading this book will help you not only to know the Ten Commandments but also to love them, delight in them, and ultimately live by them."

Jeremy Treat, Pastor for Preaching and Vision, Reality LA, Los Angeles, California; Adjunct Professor of Theology, Biola University; author, *Seek First* and *The Crucified King*

"I've studied and preached the Ten Commandments over the last thirty years, but *Ten Words to Live By* helped me to see new truths and consider fresh applications. This book is biblical, thoughtful, and deeply practical. Jen Wilkin masterfully brings the ancient summary of the law to daily life. Regardless of your background with studying the Bible, read this book. You'll be led to appreciate the Ten Commandments and how much we need them today."

Mark Vroegop, Lead Pastor, College Park Church, Indianapolis, Indiana; author, *Dark Clouds, Deep Mercy* and *Weep with Me*

Ten Words to Live By

Ten Words to Live By

Delighting in and Doing
What God Commands

Jen Wilkin

WHEATON, ILLINOIS

Ten Words to Live By: Delighting in and Doing What God Commands

Copyright © 2021 by Jen Wilkin

Published by Crossway
   1300 Crescent Street
   Wheaton, Illinois 60187

Cover Design: Crystal Courtney

First printing 2021

Printed in the United States of America

Trade paperback ISBN: 978-1-4335-6634-9
ePub ISBN: 978-1-4335-6637-0
PDF ISBN: 978-1-4335-6635-6
Mobipocket ISBN: 978-1-4335-6636-3

Library of Congress Cataloging-in-Publication Data

Names: Wilkin, Jen, 1969– author.
Title: Ten words to live by : delighting in and doing what God commands / Jen Wilkin.
Description: Wheaton, Illinois : Crossway, 2021. | Includes bibliographical references and index.
Identifiers: LCCN 2020040303 (print) | LCCN 2020040304 (ebook) | ISBN 9781433566349 (trade paperback) | ISBN 9781433566363 (pdf) | ISBN 9781433566363 (mobi) | ISBN 9781433566370 (epub)
Subjects: LCSH: Ten commandments—Criticism, interpretation, etc.
Classification: LCC BV4655 .W535 2021 (print) | LCC BV4655 (ebook) | DDC 241.5/2—dc23
LC record available at https://lccn.loc.gov/2020040303
LC ebook record available at https://lccn.loc.gov/2020040304

Crossway is a publishing ministry of Good News Publishers.

LSC   31 30 29 28 27 26 25 24 23 22 21
14 13 12 11 10 9 8 7 6 5 4 3 2

Contents

THE TEN WORDS

Exodus 20:2–17

"I am the LORD your God, who brought you out of the land of Egypt, out of the house of slavery.

✦ COMMANDMENT 1

"You shall have no other gods before me.

✦ COMMANDMENT 2

"You shall not make for yourself a carved image, or any likeness of anything that is in heaven above, or that is in the earth beneath, or that is in the water under the earth. You shall not bow down to them or serve them, for I the LORD your God am a jealous God, visiting the iniquity of the fathers on the children to the third and the fourth generation of those who hate me, but showing steadfast love to thousands of those who love me and keep my commandments.

✦ COMMANDMENT 3

"You shall not take the name of the LORD your God in vain, for the LORD will not hold him guiltless who takes his name in vain.

✤ COMMANDMENT 4

"Remember the Sabbath day, to keep it holy. Six days you shall labor, and do all your work, but the seventh day is a Sabbath to the LORD your God. On it you shall not do any work, you, or your son, or your daughter, your male servant, or your female servant, or your livestock, or the sojourner who is within your gates. For in six days the LORD made heaven and earth, the sea, and all that is in them, and rested on the seventh day. Therefore the LORD blessed the Sabbath day and made it holy.

✤ COMMANDMENT 5

"Honor your father and your mother, that your days may be long in the land that the LORD your God is giving you.

✤ COMMANDMENT 6

"You shall not murder.

✤ COMMANDMENT 7

"You shall not commit adultery.

✤ COMMANDMENT 8

"You shall not steal.

✤ COMMANDMENT 9

"You shall not bear false witness against your neighbor.

✤ COMMANDMENT 10

"You shall not covet your neighbor's house; you shall not covet your neighbor's wife, or his male servant, or his female servant, or his ox, or his donkey, or anything that is your neighbor's."

"Owe no one anything, except to love each other, for the one who loves another has fulfilled the law. For the commandments, 'You shall not commit adultery, You shall not murder, You shall not steal, You shall not covet,' and any other commandment, are summed up in this word: 'You shall love your neighbor as yourself.' Love does no wrong to a neighbor; therefore love is the fulfilling of the law."

Introduction

Remember to Delight

*For this is the love of God, that we
keep his commandments. And his
commandments are not burdensome.*

1 JOHN 5:3

THIS IS A BOOK ABOUT the law of God in all of its life-giving beauty. In the church today there exists a great forgetfulness about the role of the law in the life of the believer. This book is an exercise in remembrance.

Far back in the earliest pages of the Old Testament, in Exodus 20 and then again in Deuteronomy 5, an ancient people in a distant land were given the *aseret hadevarim*, the Ten Words. What the Torah and the rabbis called the Ten Words, you and I know as the Ten Commandments. Given to Moses on Mount Sinai, inscribed on tablets of stone by the very finger of God, these ten laws were intended to serve the Israelites as they left behind pagan Egypt and entered into pagan Canaan. They comprise the moral law of the Old Testament, undergirding its civil and ceremonial laws.

Moses assured those people, the nation of Israel, that obedience to these Ten Words would result in life and blessing:

> So be careful to do what the LORD your God has commanded you; do not turn aside to the right or to the left. Walk in obedience to all that the LORD your God has commanded you, so that you may live and prosper and prolong your days in the land that you will possess. (Deut. 5:32–33 NIV)

The Ten Commandments are perhaps the best-known example of moral law, informing law codes into modern times. Though most people know about the Ten Words, few can actually enumerate them. One well-known survey found that, while Americans struggled to recall the Ten Commandments, they could name the seven ingredients of a Big Mac and all six members of the Brady Bunch with relative ease.[1] In my experience, not many Christians are able to name the Decalogue's ten "key ingredients," either. Can you name them all? Should you be able to?

When the Ten Commandments are not forgotten, they are often wrongly perceived. They suffer from a PR problem. They are seen by many as the obsolete utterances of a thunderous, grumpy God to a disobedient people, neither of whom seem very relatable or likable. Because we have trouble seeing any beauty in the Ten Words, forgetting them comes easily.

---

1 Reuters Life!, "Americans Know Big Macs Better Than Ten Commandments," *Reuters*, Thomson Reuters, October 12, 2007, www.reuters.com/article/us-bible -commandments/americans-know-big-macs-better-than-ten-commandments-idUSN 1223894020071012.

Law and Grace

Perhaps you have heard the statement "Christianity isn't about rules, it's about relationship." It is an idea that has enjoyed popularity in recent decades, as evangelistic messages increasingly emphasized a personal relationship with God, one made possible through the grace that forgives our sins against God's law. In many ways, this evangelistic approach seeks to solve the PR problem I have noted. It trades the grumpy Old Testament God of the law for the compassionate New Testament God of grace.

Thus, law and grace have come to be pitted against one another as enemies, when in fact, they are friends. The God of the Old Testament and the God of the New have been placed in opposition, when in fact, they are one and the same. God does not change. His justice and compassion have always coexisted, and so have his law and his grace. Herein lies our forgetfulness. Rather than seeing the sin of lawlessness as the barrier to relationship with God, we have steadily grown to regard the law itself as the barrier. We have come to believe that rules prevent relationship.

So, is Christianity about rules, or is it about relationship? The Christian faith is absolutely about relationship. But while that faith is personal, it is also communal. We are saved into special relationship with God, and thereby into special relationship with other believers. Christianity is about relationship with God and others, and because this statement is true, Christianity is also unapologetically about rules, for rules show us how to live in those relationships. Rather than threaten relationship, rules enable it. We know this is true from everyday life. Imagine you are a substitute teacher at an elementary school. Which kindergarten class would you rather substitute for: the one with established and respected rules posted on the bulletin board, or the one without? Rules ensure that the one in charge is honored, and that those in her charge look to the interests of others as well as their own. Without rules, our hopes of healthy relationship vanish in short order. Jesus did not pit rules against relationship. It was he who said, "If you love me, you will keep my commandments."[2]

Christians have been taught, with good reason, to fear legalism—attempting to earn favor through obedience to the law. Legalism is a terrible blight, as evidenced in the example of the Pharisees. But in our zeal to avoid legalism, we have at times forgotten the many places the beauty of the law is extolled for us, both in the Old Testament and the New. Blessed, says the psalmist, is the one whose delight is in the law of the Lord.[3] While legalism is a blight, lawfulness is a blessed virtue, as evidenced in the example of Christ.

We should love the law because we love Jesus, and because Jesus loved the law. Contrary to common belief, the Pharisees were not lovers of the law; they were lovers of self. This is why Jesus says that unless our righteousness *exceeds* that of the scribes and Pharisees, we will never enter the kingdom of heaven (Matt. 5:20). Legalism is external righteousness only, practiced to curry favor. Legalism is not love of the law, but is its own form of lawlessness, twisting the law for its own ends.

When the Scriptures condemn lawlessness, as they repeatedly and vehemently do, they condemn both the one who ignores the law and the one who embraces it for self-righteous ends. Note

2   John 14:15
3   See Ps. 1.

the words of the apostle John: "Everyone who makes a practice of sinning also practices lawlessness; sin is lawlessness" (1 John 3:4).

The very definition of sin is rejection of law. What, then, is lawfulness?

Lawfulness is Christlikeness. To obey the law is to look like Jesus Christ. While legalism builds self-righteousness, lawfulness builds righteousness. Obedience to the law is the means of sanctification for the believer. We serve the risen Christ, "who gave himself for us to redeem us from all lawlessness and to purify for himself a people for his own possession who are zealous for good works" (Titus 2:14).

So, it is my fervent hope that this book will increase your zeal. There are good works to be done by the people of God, not out of dread to earn his favor, but out of delight because we already have it. That favor is our freedom, a freedom from slavery better understood when we remember its foreshadowing many years ago in the time of the Ten Words.

A Feast in the Wilderness

Before God speaks the law to Israel from the top of Sinai, he speaks deliverance to Moses from the burning bush. Israel was in the throes of bitter toil. Four hundred years in Egypt had rendered them slaves with no hope of freedom. But the bush speaks. Yahweh makes known his plan of great rescue. Moses is to go to Pharaoh with a request: "Please let us go a three days' journey into the wilderness, that we may sacrifice to the LORD our God" (Ex. 3:18).

Let us go. It will become the refrain of the next sixteen chapters of Exodus. Seven times, Moses will bring the words of God to

Pharaoh: "Let my people go that they may serve me, that they may make a feast to me in the wilderness" (Ex. 5:1; 7:16; 8:1, 20; 9:1, 13; 10:3).

A feast in the wilderness. An act of worship. Something heretofore out of the question. Bitter servitude to Pharaoh had made blessed service to God an impossibility for Israel. How could they serve both God and Pharaoh? Obedient worship to the King of heaven cannot be offered by those enslaved in the kingdom of Pharaoh. *Let us go.*

But Pharaoh is a stubborn master. Why would he release them to serve another master when they are serving him? With ten plagues, Yahweh breaks the rod of Pharaoh and delivers his children through passageways of blood and of water. Ten great labor pains, and a birth: the servants of Pharaoh find themselves reborn into their true identity as the servants of God. Let the feasting begin.

But hunger and thirst are their first companions, and they grumble against God. He meets their needs with living water and food from heaven, a foretaste of the provision awaiting them in Canaan. And at last they draw near to the foot of the mountain, the place God has called them to for the purpose of worship, sacrifice, and feasting.

God descends in thunder and lightning, and gives them not the feast they expect, but the feast they need. He gives them the law. The law of Pharaoh they know by heart, but the law of Yahweh is at best a distant memory to them after four hundred years in Egypt. He does not give it when they are in Egypt, for how could they serve two masters? No, instead, he waits, graciously giving it at the point they are finally able to obey. Come to the feast. Come famished by the law of Pharaoh to feast on the law of the Lord. Come taste the law that gives freedom (James 1:25).

Many years later, Jesus would speak to his followers of their own relationship to the law. *No one can serve two masters. Be born again by water and blood. Hunger and thirst for righteousness. If the Son sets you free, you will be free indeed.*[4] Jesus shows himself to be the true and better Moses, leading us to the foot of Mount Zion to trade the law of sin and death for the law of love and life.

It is for freedom that Christ, the true and better Moses, has set you free.[5] We are moved from the kingdom of darkness to the kingdom of light, from the dehumanizing law of the oppressor to the humanizing law of freedom. We find ourselves in the wilderness of testing, nourished on the bread that came down from heaven, longing for a better home. How then shall we live? Hear the words of Paul:

> For just as you once presented your members as slaves to impurity and to lawlessness leading to more lawlessness, so now present your members as slaves to righteousness leading to sanctification. (Rom. 6:19)

For those in the wilderness, the law is graciously given to set us apart from those around us, and to point the way to love of God and love of neighbor. The Ten Words show us how to live holy lives as citizens of heaven while we yet dwell on earth. For the believer, the law becomes a means of grace.

4 Matt. 5:6; 6:24; John 3:5; 8:36
5 Gal. 5:1

Encouraging Words

Rules enable relationship. The Ten Words graciously position us to live at peace with God and others. The Great Commandment, the one which Jesus says sums up all 611 of the general and specific laws of the Old Testament, bears this out:

> You shall love the Lord your God with all your heart and with all your soul and with all your strength and with all your mind, and your neighbor as yourself. (Luke 10:27)

The Great Commandment is the underlying principle for all right living. Not surprisingly, the Ten Words follow the same pattern of Godward lawfulness first, and manward lawfulness second. The Ten Words are encouraging words, meant to give us hope—hope that we will live rightly oriented to God and others, hope that we will grow in holiness.[6] They are not given to discourage but to delight. They are no less than words of life.

But take note: they are not words of life for everyone. For the unbeliever, obedience to the Ten Words can yield only the deadly fruit of legalism. As the author of Hebrews makes plain, "Without faith it is impossible to please [God]" (Heb. 11:6). These words bring life only to those who have been joined to Christ through faith. Our relationship has been purchased by the perfect obedience of Christ to the law. The life of Jesus fulfills the prophetic words of Psalm 40:8: "I delight to do your will, O my God; / your law is within my heart."

He who delighted in the law of God offers it to those who trust in him, that they might delight in it, as well. And so that

6 Rom. 15:4

they might please God. With faith, by the power of the Spirit, it is possible to please God.

I propose that we determine not just to remember the Ten Words, but to delight in them, to see beauty in them, to seek encouragement from them, and to live by them. They stand ancient and timeless, as for ransomed Israel, so for us: a feast of righteousness spread in the wilderness, fortifying our hearts for the journey home.

1

The First Word

Undivided Allegiance

being loyal

> *And God spoke all these words, saying, "I am the LORD your God, who brought you out of the land of Egypt, out of the house of slavery. You shall have no other gods before me."*
>
> EXODUS 20:1–3

EVEN AS A LIFE-LONG TEXAN, I can acknowledge that Texas is a funny and wonderful place. We decorate our homes and yards with Texas flags and Texas-themed artwork. By the time our children graduate from high school, they will have studied Texas history for two solid years. They will have sung our superlative-laden state song ("Texas, our Texas! All hail the mighty State!") at every high school football game and every major sporting event. Not only that, but in addition to pledging allegiance to the American flag, they will have begun each school day by honoring the Texas flag: "I pledge allegiance to thee, Texas, one state under God, one and indivisible."

I don't hear similar fervor from those from other states, decorative or declarative. I suspect that is because Texans take pride in the unique fact that we inhabit the only state that was once a nation unto itself. The War of Texas Independence was kind of a big deal for us. Do we remember the Alamo? Yes . . . yes, we do.

Remembering a history of a costly liberation shapes the Texas psyche. Pledging allegiance to our state—and our country—reminds us that we all owe our duty to an authority greater than ourselves. We understand ourselves to be in submission to those who make the laws, and therefore to the laws themselves.

The same was true of Israel, and the same is true of every follower of the one true God. The reality of a higher authority explains why the giving of the Ten Commandments doesn't actually begin with the utterance of the first commandment. Instead it begins with a brief history lesson recalling a costly liberation and establishing who is in charge: "And God spoke all these words, saying, 'I am the LORD your God, who brought you out of the land of Egypt, out of the house of slavery'" (Ex. 20:1–2).

A mere fifty days earlier, Israel had departed Egypt in the wake of the ten plagues sent to accomplish her release. Fresh in their minds would be the memory of those dark days—the Nile running thickly red, dead frogs heaped in stinking piles, swarms of blighting insects, hail, diseases, darkness, and death. Having gathered them at Mount Sinai, in thunder and smoke God reminds his people that it was by his mighty hand alone that their liberation was accomplished. Israel's only contribution to her freedom was to arise in obedience, as those walking from death to life. God introduces the Ten Commandments to his people by identifying himself as the Lord *their God* and prompting them with "Remember Egypt." Why? Because before Israel can pledge allegiance to Yahweh alone, she must recall her costly deliverance.

That deliverance entailed not just leaving behind the land of Egypt, but leaving behind the ways of Egypt. Each of the ten plagues was more than just a dramatic sign to Pharaoh that he must release the Hebrews. Each was a symbolic defeat of an Egyptian deity. Osiris, whose bloodstream was believed to be the Nile, bleeds out before his worshipers when Yahweh turns the Nile to blood. In reverence to Heqet, the frog-goddess of birth, Egyptians regarded frogs as sacred and not to be killed. Yahweh slays them by the thousands. Egyptian gods governing fertility, crops, live-stock, and health are all shown to be impotent before the mighty outstretched arm of Israel's God. In the ninth plague of darkness, Yahweh demonstrates his rule over the sun god Ra, whom Pharaoh was believed to embody. And in the final plague, the death of the firstborn, God shows himself supreme over the entire Egyptian pantheon by demonstrating his power over life and death.

One God toppling all rivals.

I am the Lord your God, who brought you out of Egypt. The message to the Israelites at the foot of Mount Sinai is clear: before you can obey me as the God of the Ten Words of life, you must revere me as the God of the ten plagues of death. The response required is obvious, too. If the God who toppled all rivals in Egypt has brought you out of Egypt by his mighty outstretched arm, the only logical response is to obey the first word: "You shall have no other gods before me."

Remember your costly deliverance. Pledge allegiance to me alone.

Only One God

The first commandment, "You shall have no other gods before me," is spoken in the language of a sovereign to a servant. There can be no dual allegiances when it comes to serving Yahweh. By commanding a singular allegiance, God does not merely assert that he is superior to other gods. Nor, in the plagues, does he merely demonstrate that he is stronger than other gods. He declares that they do not exist. They are nothing more than the vain imaginings of a darkened mind. The first word is more than a prohibition against worshiping lesser gods; it is an invitation into reality. "I am the LORD, and there is no other, / besides me there is no God" (Isa. 45:5). Why should Israel worship no other gods before God? Because there are no other gods.

Maybe that seems obvious. God has just routed his people's greatest enemy and put their nonexistent gods to shame. But the truth that there is only one God to be worshiped must settle deep into the bones of the people of Israel, for God has brought his children victoriously out of polytheistic Egypt for the purpose of leading them victoriously into polytheistic Canaan.

After four hundred years in Egypt, polytheism would be more familiar to Israel than the monotheism the first word expresses. It would feel more natural than the singular worship God commands, as sin in comparison to righteousness so often does. The land just across the Jordan beckons with the comfortable familiarity of many-god worship. The likelihood that Israel would return to the familiar is high.

The call to monotheism would not be a new idea to Israel at the foot of Sinai. The creation account of Genesis 1 contains the implicit command to worship only God. Like the ten plagues, the six days of creation are purposely worded to topple any notion of worshiping sun, moon, stars, earth, sea, sky, plants, animals, or humans. All of the heavens and earth are shown to be derivative, dependent upon, and in service to the God without origin who effortlessly speaks them into existence.

But God's people forget that pretty quickly. As early as chapter 35 of Genesis, we encounter a cautionary tale of divided worship among the children of God. It seems that between his exile in Paddan Aram and his return to Bethel, Jacob and his family had picked up a few household idol stowaways in their saddlebags. Though God has not explicitly commanded it, Jacob knows the idols must go:

> So Jacob said to his household and to all who were with him, "Get rid of the foreign gods you have with you, and purify yourselves and change your clothes. Then come, let us go up to Bethel, where I will build an altar to God, who answered me in the day of my distress and who has been with me wherever I have gone." (Gen. 35:2–3 NIV)

The presence of idols among Jacob's family points to the operation of a "both-and" mentality: yes, we will serve Yahweh, but also, just in case, we will offer devotion to these other gods, as well.

Dual allegiance. Can you relate?

This mentality hides in the baggage of believers today just as it did in Jacob's family three thousand years ago. It's an age-old expression of what James 1:8 refers to as double-mindedness. Double-mindedness occurs not because we *replace* God with an idol, but because we *add* an idol to our *mono*theon so that it becomes a *poly*theon. The repeated refrain on idolatry throughout Israel's history will not be that she ceases worship of God *entirely*, but that she ceases worship of God *alone*.

An Expansive Obedience

The children of Yahweh today are not so different from the children of Yahweh then. Like Israel, we affirm that there are no other gods verbally and intellectually, but not practically. Practically, we live as polytheists. Our idolatry is a "both-and" arrangement: I need God *and* I need a spouse. I need God *and* I need a smaller waist size. I need God *and* I need good health. I need God *and* I need a well-padded bank account.

In our minds, we rationalize that the "both-and" still offers God some form or degree of worship, so everything must be okay. Yet, according to Genesis and Exodus, to cease to worship God alone is to corrupt any worship still offered to him.

In Matthew 6:24, Jesus teaches us that "no one can serve two masters, for either he will hate the one and love the other, or he will be devoted to the one and despise the other." We may think dual allegiance is desirable, but Jesus assures us it is not even possible. We are created for single-minded allegiance. We are designed for it. We are made in the image of one God, to bear the image of one God. We cannot conform to both the image of God and the image of an idol.

We are not designed to be polytheists, nor can we sustain the weight of a many-God lie in our minds. When we cling to God-and-_____, we become "unstable in all [our] ways" (James 1:8).

It often takes a crisis to point out our folly. There is nothing like a financial crisis to teach us our worship of money and comfort in addition to God. There is nothing like a wayward child or a divorce to teach us our worship of having a perfect family in addition to God. There is nothing like the aging process to teach us our worship of health and beauty in addition to God.

It is at just such a crisis point that we find Jacob ready to expel the household idols. Penitent, he has just come face-to-face with his own failures. His daughter had been violated, and his sons had responded with terrible vengeance when he himself failed to seek justice. Jacob is a man broken of his self-reliance and soured on his own cunning. He is a man familiar with crisis. He is a man at last learning to pledge allegiance to God alone.

Whatever instability may be needed to bring us to repentance, the final solution to our practice of polytheism is found in Jacob's story: "So they gave Jacob all the foreign gods they had and the rings in their ears, and Jacob buried them under the oak at Shechem" (Gen. 35:4 NIV).

Jacob could have destroyed the idols in any way. He might have burned them, thrown them in a lake, or hacked them to bits. Instead, he buries them under a landmark tree known as a place of idol worship. Determined to put the past behind him and live in the truth that God is his only hope, Jacob symbolically holds a funeral for the idols in the very place they were typically worshiped.[1] With pointed irony, the place for idol worship symbolically becomes a burial ground for it.

Do not miss the moral of the story: to rid ourselves of our idols, we must put them to death.

---

1   Bill T. Arnold, *Encountering the Book of Genesis* (Grand Rapids, MI: Baker, 2004), 137.

Burying Our Both-Ands

Jacob holds a necessary funeral, and so must we. The apostle Paul urges us to do so:

Put to death therefore what is earthly in you: sexual immorality, impurity, passion, evil desire, and covetousness, *which is idolatry*. On account of these the wrath of God is coming. In these you too once walked, when you were living in them. But now you must put them all away: anger, wrath, malice, slander, and obscene talk from your mouth. Do not lie to one another, seeing that you have put off the old self with its practices and have put on the new self, which is being renewed in knowledge after the image of its creator. (Col. 3:5–10)

Notice Paul describes a list of idolatrous behaviors quite similar to the sins we will find forbidden in the Ten Words. Paul does not mean for us to put to death behaviors only, but the idols of the heart that hide behind them. He is urging believers to be students of our behaviors as indicators of what (or who) we worship in addition to God.

The first word serves as the umbrella statement for the other nine. If we obeyed the first word, we would automatically obey the others. It establishes the proper posture before God that enables the proper motives and behaviors to obey the other nine.

We were created in the image of God. The more we worship an idol, the more we will conform to its image. To put to death an idol is to be restored to the image of God.

Like Jacob, we must bury our idols. By the power of the Spirit, we must bury our both-ands, and keep them buried, learning from our past mistakes and growing in righteousness with each passing day. The first word prepares us for the other nine by demanding our undivided allegiance to the God of our costly deliverance. Without that pledge on our lips and in our hearts, all obedience to the commands that follow will be an exercise in empty moralism. The first word is a pledge of allegiance to the kingdom of God, here and now.

On Earth as in Heaven

Remember how it all began? In Eden, the first commandment was perfectly validated and perfectly obeyed. In that pure haven for that brief interlude, there were no other gods before God. Image bearers bore his image undiluted and undefiled. But dual allegiances sprang from the double-tongued lisping of the serpent. Adam and Eve succumbed to the lure of God-and-fill-in-the-blank, and Eden's pure worship was lost. We feel the loss of it every day—battling for single-minded devotion, seeking to obey as our single-minded Savior taught us and showed us to obey.

One day his kingdom will come in fullness, on earth as it is in heaven. That day, single-minded and whole-hearted allegiance will be fully restored. In the New Jerusalem, we will at last and once again have no other gods before him. The apostle John describes for us what this final haven will look like:

> The wall was built of jasper, while the city was pure gold, like clear glass. The foundations of the wall of the city were adorned with every kind of jewel. . . . And the city has no need of sun or moon to shine on it, for the glory of God gives it light, and its lamp is the Lamb. (Rev. 21:18–19, 23)

It's quite an eye-popping description.[2] At first glance, it seems that pearly gates, gem-encrusted walls, and streets made of gold are meant to stir our excitement to live in a place where opulence abounds at every level—a place so splendid that it outshines the sun. But John's description of the New Jerusalem is meant to tell us something more. It takes the things we esteem the highest in this life and reduces them to the level of commonplace. All of these elements—gold, precious stones, the celestial bodies, rulers, crowns—are what humans throughout history have worshiped, the stuff of our dual allegiances. These are the idols of this world.

The New Jerusalem is a first-is-last place, where the things we have exalted will be cast down to the level of their real worth: as mere metal and stone, as mere human authority, as mere created lights that move at the command of their Creator. It is a place where precious metals and stones are trodden under foot as common road dust, where our crowning personal honors are cast at God's feet, where the people and objects and institutions to which we have ascribed our worship will fall from their lofty places.

It is a place whose inhabitants at last obey the first word: "You shall have no other gods before me." It is Eden restored.

Jesus, who kept the first word in every way, taught his followers to pray that God's kingdom might come "on earth as it is in heaven" (Matt. 6:10). Why wait until the next life to count

---

2 Portions of the following first appeared in my article "Heaven Shines, But Who Cares?" ChristianityToday.com, August 20, 2020, https://www.christianitytoday.com/ct/2018 /september/wilkin-heaven-shines-but-who-cares.html.

as worthless what God counts as worthless? Why wait until the next life to esteem what God esteems? The first word invites us into the blessed reality of no other gods *now*. It is our undiluted worship that marks us as his children in a crooked and depraved generation.

Today is the day for toppling our idols of power, wealth, security, and comfort. Now is the time for treading in the dust the gods of our sinful desires. To live this life unbound to the things of earth is to anticipate the indescribable joy of an eternity in which every earthly pleasure bows to the pleasure of being finally and fully in the presence of the one and only God. Choose this day whom you will serve. Pledge your allegiance.

Verses for Meditation

Psalm 86:10–12 - *Teach me your way.*
Isaiah 45:5 - *I am the Lord*
Matthew 6:24 *serve two masters (no one)*
Colossians 3:5–10 *Take off old self - (new self)*
James 1:6–8 *believe - not doubt*
Revelation 15:4 *fear you*

Questions for Reflection

1. Before reading this chapter, how would you have rated your obedience to the first commandment? After reading it, how would you rate yourself? What insight accounts for the change in your diagnosis?

2. What idol are you most tempted to worship alongside God? What are you hoping to control or avoid by this dual allegiance?

3. What current sinful behavior can you trace to worshiping something alongside God? How does forgetfulness of your costly deliverance factor into the way you respond to temptation?

4. In the introduction, it was noted that laws help us live in community. How does the first word help the children of God to live in community with one another? How does double-mindedness harm Christian community?

Write a prayer asking God to help you to obey the first commandment. Confess where you have harbored dual allegiances and worshiped other gods of your imagining. Ask him to help you live as a citizen of his kingdom today and every day. Praise him that he is God unrivaled. Thank him for your costly deliverance.

2

The Second Word

Undiminished Worship

*"You shall not make for yourself a carved image, or
any likeness of anything that is in heaven above, or
that is in the earth beneath, or that is in the water
under the earth. You shall not bow down to them or
serve them, for I the LORD your God am a jealous
God, visiting the iniquity of the fathers on the children
to the third and the fourth generation of those who
hate me, but showing steadfast love to thousands of
those who love me and keep my commandments."*

EXODUS 20:4–6

AFTER A BRIEF DECLARATION that God and God alone is to
be worshiped, the second word goes into some detail about the
power and danger of image making. It forbids exhaustively the
making of an image of anything in God's creation—celestial,
terrestrial, or otherwise. It forbids explicitly the offering of our

worship to anything of the kind, complete with a warning of the grave consequences that will result.

The second word portrays idol worship as progressive: do not make, do not bow down, do not serve. The second word portrays idol worship as contagious, causing trouble for generation after generation. The second word portrays God as zealous for his glory: deeply committed to being worshiped as he deserves. His jealousy is right and righteous because it is inflamed by the denial of what is rightly his. His steadfast love is shown to the obedient.

But surely this command is redundant? Hasn't idolatry already been explored in the first word? Whereas the first word addressed idolatry in general, the second now addresses it in a more specific form: we should not make images of created things and worship them as the Creator. The second word helps us understand the relationship between visible images and an invisible God.

God determines what is acceptable worship. Making an image to represent him is out of bounds, and for good reason, as we will see. It's important to note that by breaking the second word, we reveal that we have also broken the first. By exercising the desire to worship God in a way contrary to his command, we set ourselves in his place, thus making ourselves God. Every transgression of one of the Ten Words begins by transgressing the first, to have no other gods before him.

At first blush, breaking the second commandment seems easy to avoid. What could be simpler than this? Just don't whittle or paint or carve anything, or worship anything whittled or painted or carved, and we're good. But like the first, the second word is calling us to a deeper obedience, one that will press us to examine what it means to recognize truth from falsehood, accurate images from inaccurate ones, and ultimately, image bearing from image management.

Photoshop Is Not New

If there is anything ubiquitous to the halls of power, certainly image management tops the list. Those who wield positions of authority are careful to ensure that we see them in the light of their choosing. Politicians running for office choose their clothing with care, even down to the cut of a dress or the color of a tie. It's always been this way. Though disabled by polio, Franklin D. Roosevelt required that the press not photograph him in a wheelchair, walking, getting into his car, or approaching a podium.[1] FDR's Secret Service ensured he retained a singular image of strength. But perhaps no other ruler has understood the importance of image management quite like Queen Elizabeth I of England.

Ascending to the throne at the age of twenty-five, she ruled for forty-four years during a time of great political upheaval. Three years into her reign, smallpox left her with facial scars and partial baldness for the rest of her life. As she aged, she lost so many teeth that her speech became impaired. But in the portraits painted of her during her lifetime, she is eternally youthful and beautiful. Why? Because she decreed that it should be so. Her secretary of state, Sir Robert Cecil, wrote:

> Many painters have done portraits of the Queen but none has sufficiently shown her looks or charms. Therefore Her Majesty

---

[1] Amy Berish, "FDR and Polio," Franklin D. Roosevelt Presidential Library and Museum website, accessed July 23, 2020, https://fdrlibrary.org/polio/.

commands all manner of persons to stop doing portraits of her until a clever painter has finished one which all other painters can copy. Her Majesty, in the meantime, forbids the showing of any portraits which are ugly until they are improved.[2]

A face template was developed, coined "the Mask of Youth," and all portrait artists were required to adhere to its standards. In a time when feminine youth implied the fertility necessary to produce an heir, Elizabeth shrewdly guarded her rule through careful image management.[3]

God's approach to image management is quite different from that of earthly rulers. Whereas earthly rulers may be compelled to wear a mask to guard their power, our heavenly ruler rejects all distortions of his image as impediments to being rightly worshiped. In order to preserve the reality of his perfections, God decrees that no human-contrived image of him shall be made, as any such image would only serve to cloud or diminish our understanding of what he is truly like. Because he is infinite and invisible, any finite and visible rendering of him in wood, paint, or plaster can only dim our understanding of his true nature. God's version of image management is that there are to be no images of him conceived by human minds and created by human hands, in order to preserve the reality of his perfections.

2   Meilan Solly, "What Did Elizabeth I Actually Look Like? This Artist Has a Suggestion," *Smithsonian Magazine*, October 16, 2018, https://www.smithsonianmag.com/smart -news/what-did-elizabeth-i-actually-look-artist-has-suggestion-180970553/#3RR4 yFjhVzSsL444.99.

3   Amy Moore, "The Image of Power? Queen Elizabeth I and the 'Mask of Youth,'" National Trust, October 23, 2017, https://www.nationaltrust.org.uk/features/the -image-of-power-queen-elizabeth-i-and-the-mask-of-youth/.

Worshiping a Lie

The first word prohibits worship of anything *other than* God, but the second prohibits worship of any version of God *less than* God, specifically through images. We are given an object lesson in the dangerous foolishness of "less-than-God God-worship" even before the second word is set in stone.

Shockingly, in between God's announcement of the Ten Commandments and the time Moses descends from Sinai with them engraved on tablets of stone, Israel decides to break the second commandment. How? By making a golden calf and bowing down to it. We find the story in Exodus 32.

Moses is called to the top of Sinai by God, but when his time there grows lengthy, the people grow restless waiting for his return. Supposing their leader has been swallowed by Sinai's thunder and smoke, they demand that Aaron make them gods to "go before" them (Ex. 32:1). Aaron obliges by collecting the gold jewelry they have presumably just lifted from the Egyptians—gold that God intended to be used in constructing his tabernacle—and embarking on a little sculpting project:[4]

> And [Aaron] received the gold from [the people's] hand and fashioned it with a graving tool and made a golden calf. And they said, "These are your gods, O Israel, who brought you up out of the land of Egypt!" When Aaron saw this, he built an altar before it. And Aaron made a proclamation and said, "Tomorrow shall be a feast to [Yahweh]." And they rose up early the next day and offered burnt offerings and brought

4   Ex. 3:22; 12:35–36

peace offerings. And the people sat down to eat and drink and rose up to play. (Ex. 32:4–6)

Interestingly, Aaron seems to conceive of the golden calf as an image of Yahweh, not as a lesser or different deity.[5] This is evident in the way he describes and executes the feast day. Israel feasts and sacrifices before an image purported to be of the one true God. But the calf can't be that. The image lies about who God truly is. Think about the enormity of the lie the golden calf tells:

It is small, but God is immense.
It is inanimate, but God is Spirit.
It is location-bound, but God is everywhere fully present.
It is created, but God is uncreated.
It is new, but God is eternal.
It is impotent, but God is omnipotent.
It is destructible, but God is indestructible.
It is of minor value, but God is of infinite value.
It is blind and deaf and mute, but God sees, hears, and speaks.

This image is no Yahweh. This is a lie. But it's a particularly pernicious kind of lie, or perhaps it is the most common kind of all. Have you ever wondered why Aaron chooses the image of a calf instead of some other animal, like a bird or a lion? Remember that Israel is in the in-between space, fresh from Egypt and heading to

5   R. C. Sproul Jr. "You Shall Not Make for Yourselves a Carved Image," *Tabletalk*, June 19, 2018, https://www.ligonier.org/learn/articles/you-shall-not-make-yourselves -carved-image/.

Canaan. One of the principal deities of Egypt was the bull god Apis, and the supreme head of the Canaanite pantheon was the bull god El. Bull-worship was all the rage in the region. But it is a knobby-kneed calf, not a raging bull, that Aaron manufactures. When Aaron conceives of a Yahweh-of-his-own-imagining, he produces a nonthreatening, approachable version of the principal gods of the surrounding pagans.

And so do we.

Any time we take the attributes of the gods the world around us worships and apply them to God to make him more palatable and less threatening, more accommodating and less thunderous, we produce a graven image. We whittle down his transcendence, we paint over his sovereignty, we chisel away his omnipotence until he is a pet-like version of the terrible pagan god we would never be so foolish as to bow down to.

Take, for example, the God of the prosperity gospel. Who among us would worship wealth when the Bible speaks so clearly of that dangerous idol, and when we see our unbelieving neighbors spend their lives chasing the almighty dollar, never to be satisfied by it? "Let us avoid that path, Lord," we pray. But instead, we go right ahead and fashion Yahweh into a benign, benevolent form of Mammon. When our finances are tight, we ask, "What lack of faith has withheld God's bounty from me?" When our bank accounts are full, we think, "It is because my faith has pleased the Lord."

Or perhaps we have rejected wholeheartedly the works-based salvation of other religions. The Muslim or the Hindu may seek to earn God's favor through moral behavior, striving all their lives to obligate God to accept them. "Let us avoid that path, Lord," we pray. But instead, we go right ahead and fashion Yahweh into a god who is obligated to reward our wise choices with blessing, who answers our properly worded "in Jesus's name" prayers as we have commanded him to. When our circumstances are grim, we ask, "Why, Lord? What did I do to deserve this?" And when they are sunny, we think, "It is because my obedience has pleased the Lord."

Or perhaps we simply take the God of the Bible and treat him according to our preferences, by placing emphasis on one of his (more palatable) attributes to the neglect of others. We speak incessantly of his love, but we grow silent about his wrath. We meditate on his grace, but we avoid contemplation of his justice. Or we trumpet his justice selectively, to suit our personal or political agendas. Perhaps we diminish his triune nature, choosing one member of the Trinity as our favorite in our prayers, our thoughts, our preaching, and our song, and forgetting the other two. We turn him into a mascot for our own ends.

Exposing the Golden Calf

A golden calf is a false teacher: it reveals to us only *God-diminished*—with a twist of phrase, a clouded lens, or a misplaced emphasis. The antidote to a false teaching is a true one. If you were to tell me that the Grand Canyon was only three miles wide, I would know you were wrong because I have stood at its edge and seen the expanse. If you were to tell me that the moon was made of cheese, I would know you were wrong because NASA has gone to great lengths to confirm otherwise. We may be just like Israel, willing to worship an image of God that can never truly show him to us. But we are not without resources to obey the second command. We are only easily lured into wrong belief about God when we are unschooled in right belief about him. We can spot a false teaching when we know the truth.

God has chosen to reveal himself through the Scriptures and through Christ. We know the truth about who God is by becoming acquainted with this revelation, by learning the Bible, and by measuring all teaching against his word. And we know the truth about who God is through Christ, the spiritually undiminished image bearer. False teaching has been the shipwreck of the faith of many. But truth remembered is the way of life. We must cling to the rock of divine revelation like our lives depend upon it, because they do.

Truth Remembered, Truth Lived

Obeying the second word is more than just remembering truth and denying false teaching. It is also living in truth. When we look past what the command prohibits to what it exhorts, we find that we actually do have some whittling to do after all.

While no creation of human ingenuity can image God faithfully, there is a creation of divine ingenuity that can. Genesis 1:26–27 explains why God forbids making idols in his image:

> Then God said, "Let us make humankind in our image, after our likeness, so they may rule over the fish of the sea and the birds of the air, over the cattle, and over all the earth, and over all the creatures that move on the earth."

> God created humankind in his own image,
> in the image of God he created them,
> male and female he created them. (NET)

41

God and God alone is permitted to make a graven image of himself. He has done so in humanity. We must not make images of God because we ourselves bear the image of God. But because of sin, we do so in a diminished way. No one has imaged God perfectly, except one: "He is the image of the invisible God, the firstborn of all creation" (Col. 1:15).

But by the power of the Spirit, grace-fueled obedience refashions us into faithful likenesses. As we put to death sin, we whittle away at what does not reflect God. As we grow in our obedience, we rechisel what has been obscured. As we cultivate inner righteousness, we polish away the tarnish keeping us from radiating the truth of the gospel. And when we look to Christ, imitating him, we begin to see restored what sin has diminished. Bearing the image of God does not mean we look like him in physical terms but rather in spiritual terms—not so that others may worship us, but so that they may worship him.

Christ, the perfect graven image of God, had "no beauty or majesty to attract us to him, / nothing in his appearance that we should desire him" (Isa. 53:2 NIV). Physically he is unremarkable, but spiritually he is the undiminished image bearer. Yet we are consumed with outward appearances. To obey the second word is to turn from worshiping lesser versions of God, and to worship God in spirit and truth. Inwardly, our spirits are renewed in his image as we witness and obey the truth of his word.

On Earth as in Heaven

In the book of Revelation, John describes his vision of the end of all things. In twenty-two chapters, he uses the phrase, "I saw" thirty-three times. He sees lampstands and bowls and beasts and elders, dragons and lambs and riders on white horses. We would expect the language of seeing to be used in a book of prophecy, but it occurs more times in Revelation than in all of the Old Testament prophetic books combined. The culmination of John's "seeing" occurs in chapter 21, where he witnesses the descent of the New Jerusalem and God seated on the throne, declaring that all things are being made new.

On the day God makes all things new, we will finally see him, and we will finally reflect him perfectly, as we were created to do. The time of seeing is not yet. In this life, we abide by the watchword that those who have not seen, and yet believe, are blessed.[6] *We shall behold him, face to face, in all of his glory.* All lesser versions of him that we have created, whether physically or mentally, will topple.

Until that time of faith becoming sight, we strive to look like Christ. If there is to be whittling, let it be the whittling away of our sins of commission. If there is to be carving, let it be the carving out of our sins of omission. The Ten Words show us how to live on earth as in heaven, conforming to the image of Christ as representatives of Yahweh. They are engraving tools. The more we obey them, the more we reflect his character, visibly, to a world that very much needs us to.

The second word compels us both to stop worshiping the image of *God-diminished,* and to start becoming the image of *God-restored.* When we fear the Lord, undiminished, we develop love, joy, peace, patience, kindness, goodness, faithfulness,

6 John 20:29

gentleness, and self-control.[7] His law becomes increasingly engraved on our hearts. And we become the graven images he created us to be.

Verses for Meditation
Genesis 1:26–27
Psalm 115:2–8
Romans 8:29
Colossians 1:15–20
Colossians 2:6–10

Questions for Reflection

1. Before reading this chapter, how would you have rated your obedience to the second commandment? After reading it, how would you rate yourself? What insight accounts for the change in your diagnosis?

2. What false teaching have you encountered firsthand that diminishes God? How does the Bible correct that false teaching?

3. Which attribute of God are you most tempted to emphasize? Which are you most tempted to diminish? What motive can you discern behind those temptations?

4. What aspect of external image management are you most prone to indulge? What aspect of internal image bearing most needs your prayer and attention?

---

7 Gal. 5:22–23

Write a prayer asking God to help you to obey the second commandment. Confess where you have fallen short by worshiping a diminished version of him. Ask him to help you to see him clearly in his word. Praise him that he cannot be contained or described by anything made by human hands. Thank him for creating you in his image.

3

The Third Word

Untarnished Name

Jane
Vocation

> *"You shall not take the name of the LORD your*
> *God in vain, for the LORD will not hold him*
> *guiltless who takes his name in vain."*

EXODUS 20:7

WE HAVE SEEN HOW the second word guards against small thoughts about God's character. The third word will take us deeper still into right worship. If the second word forbids low or careless *thoughts* about God, the third forbids low or careless *words* about God. Like the second commandment, at first blush the third seems an easy one to avoid breaking: just don't swear, right? Or even more generously understood (for those who indulge in the occasional choice term when they stub a toe or are cut off in traffic), just don't swear using the name of God. Simple. On to the fourth commandment.

But as we have seen with the first two words, the third points us beyond bare-minimum obedience to abundant life. If all that was at stake was literal name usage, we could check off compliance with the third word by applying minor self-control. But names in the Bible do more than just identify an individual. Therein lies the key to the deeper obedience of the third word.

What's in a Name?

Do you know what your name means? In modern Western culture, parents commonly select names for their children based on personal preference. We name our children after a relative or significant person, or according to a popularity trend, or just because we like the way a name sounds. I can speak to the popularity trend with some level of expertise, having been born during an era now referred to as the Jennifer Epidemic, a period during which my given name reigned unchallenged atop the list of baby girl names for an unprecedented fourteen solid years.[1] We Jennifers are everywhere. And we are all roughly the same age. Though I am Irish, my name traces to a Welsh origin, meaning "white wave." My mother had no idea of its meaning when she named me. When I asked her why she chose it, she said, "I just liked the way it sounded, and I didn't know any other babies named Jennifer."

As it turns out, there were just a few (million) others.

Unlike current naming practices, in the ancient Near East the giving of a name was deeply significant. A name carried a sense

---

1   Jen Gerson, "The Jennifer Epidemic: How the Spiking Popularity of Different Baby Names Cycle Like Genetic Drift," *National Post*, January 26, 2015, https://national post.com/news/the-jennifer-epidemic-how-the-spiking-popularity-of-different-baby -names-cycle-like-genetic-drift/.

of the person's character, whether good or bad. Jacob's name literally means "he grasps the heel," but as his story develops, his name becomes synonymous with the idea of deceit and grasping for control. In 1 Samuel we meet Nabal, whose name means "perverse fool," and he is indeed just that in his dealings with David and Abigail. Joshua's name means "Yahweh is salvation," and it represents his character and purpose well. It is the root of the name *Jesus*.

So, what does the Bible mean when it speaks of "the name of the Lord"? Any time we hear of "the name of the Lord" in a verse or passage, we can substitute "the character of the Lord" in its place. God's name represents the sum total of his character. He is holy, loving, just, compassionate, omnipresent, omnipotent, sovereign, gracious, merciful, patient, infinite, and good. To pray "in the name of the Lord" is to pray according to his character. To call upon the name of the Lord is to ask God to act according to his character. To take shelter in the name of the Lord is to place our trust in who he is. To be baptized in the name of the Lord is to identify with his character as our salvation, our strength, and our new identity.

To misuse the name of the Lord—to take his name in vain—is to misrepresent the character of God. The NIV reads this way: "You shall not misuse the name of the LORD your God." The general sense of the Hebrew is that we are not to "lift up" the name of Yahweh to falsehood.[2] We are not to associate God's name with falsehood about his character. Doing so misuses his

---

2   Bruce K. Waltke, *An Old Testament Theology: An Exegetical, Canonical, and Thematic Approach* (Grand Rapids, MI: Zondervan, 2008), 419.

reputation to suit our own ends, speaks of or to him without accuracy or due respect, and miscredits him for self-serving actions done in his name. To misuse the name of God is to commit an act of defamation against Yahweh himself.

We do so, often unthinkingly, through everyday patterns of speech, using the name of the Lord with inconsistency, misattribution, lip service, and informality.

The Sin of Inconsistency

Have you ever followed up a story with, "I swear, that's exactly what happened"? Have you ever run late on a deadline and said, "I swear I'll get it done by Friday"? When we fear a deficit is perceived in our character or our resolve, we tend to bolster our words by swearing oaths. In the Sermon on the Mount, Jesus notes and corrects this tendency to enhance the credibility of our weak words by appealing to a higher power as witness:

> Again you have heard that it was said to those of old, "You shall not swear falsely, but shall perform to the Lord what you have sworn." But I say to you, Do not take an oath at all, either by heaven, for it is the throne of God, or by the earth, for it is his footstool, or by Jerusalem, for it is the city of the great King. And do not take an oath by your head, for you cannot make one hair white or black. Let what you say be simply "Yes" or "No"; anything more than this comes from evil. (Matt. 5:33–37)

Jesus's words in the Sermon on the Mount expand his listeners' understanding of a commandment already given to them in

Leviticus 19:12: "You shall not swear by my name falsely, and so profane the name of your God: I am the LORD." Jesus indicates that we profane the name of God not just when we swear with phrases like "As God is my witness" or "I swear to God," but any time we use an oath of any kind to enhance credibility. Jesus asserts that God's children should be so known for their integrity in all their speech and dealings that no further word is needed beyond our yes or our no. No need to call God to witness our words; the God of heaven and earth stands witness to every word we will ever speak. Indeed, he knows them all before they are formed on our tongues, and we will give an account for all of them (Ps. 139:4; Matt. 12:36–37).

Instead, we should state our commitments and fulfill them. When we speak with integrity, we fulfill the third word. We represent a truthful and faithful God accurately in our truthful speech and in our faithfulness to do what we say we will do.

The Sin of Misattribution

If the sin of inconsistency is to garner legitimacy for what we promise to do, the sin of misattribution is to garner legitimacy for what we are doing or have done. We make our own plan and execute it in the name of God, trading on his reputation to gain support for the direction we have devised. We baptize human agendas with heavenly endorsement. Or, to use the common expression, we "play the God card."

History is filled with grand-scale examples of Christians using God and the Bible to justify their own agendas. The so-called "Hamite curse" of Genesis 9:18–27 has been misused by Christians to justify both the persecution of Muslims and African chattel slavery.[3] The Crusades of the Middle Ages were similarly baptized with crooked theology to justify a political expansion of power and territory.

But aggressions against the reputation of God are uttered in his name on a smaller scale on a regular basis. Has wise counsel questioned your plans? Just tell them that "God told you" this was the direction to take. Not interested in taking on a ministry opportunity? Just say you need to pray about it, and then a few days later say you sensed the Lord calling you in another direction. Need to add punch to your political view? Be sure to attach the word *biblical* to it in a way that implies all other positions are not. The sin of misattribution is the perfect smokescreen, presenting as piety and humility while masking pride and hypocrisy.

Christians also commit the sin of misattribution when we speak of God's blessing only in terms of positive events. We tend to attribute sunshine to God and storm to Satan. But in Genesis 50, Joseph gives us an example of obedience to the third commandment. No doubt, his treatment at the hands of his brothers was unjust and, yes, satanic, but in hindsight he attributes God's sovereignty as the means of bringing blessing even from terrible trial: "As for you, you meant evil against me, but God meant it for good" (Gen. 50:20).

But perhaps the most chilling form of misattribution is when we blame God for our own sin. Just as Adam pinned his fruit-eating ways on "the woman *whom you gave me*," we too can misattribute our guilt to God.[4] This family *that you gave me* causes my

---

3   Felicia R. Lee, "From Noah's Curse to Slavery's Rationale," *The New York Times*, November 01, 2003, https://www.nytimes.com/2003/11/01/arts/from-noah-s-curse-to-slavery-s-rationale.html.

4   Gen. 3:12 (NET)

anger to flair. This job *that you gave me* causes me to neglect my relationships. This house *that you gave* me tempts me to spend money frivolously. This body *that you gave me* feeds my pride or self-loathing.

Instead of misattributing and playing either the viceroy or the victim of God, we should take responsibility for our decisions. When our words and character clearly demonstrate godly wisdom, we do not need to say "thus saith the Lord" to give them added punch. When we acknowledge God's sovereignty behind both our highs and our lows, we speak as the Bible speaks. We represent a just God accurately by affirming both human responsibility for sin and divine sovereignty over all things, good and bad.

The Sin of Lip Service

We can also misuse the name of the Lord by speaking hallowed words while living hollow lives. When we preach a moral code that we ourselves do not strive to uphold, we become like those Jesus railed against during his ministry—a people who honor God with our lips, but whose hearts are far from him.[5] This is the parent who requires her child to apologize to her, but who never apologizes for her own missteps. It is the mentor who dispenses godly wisdom to a younger believer that he has not himself learned to employ. It is the woman singing praise songs at the top of her lungs, eyes closed and hands extended, who has not cracked open her Bible in months. It is the man who prays publicly with great piety and eloquence but whose private prayer life is nonexistent. It is the greeter at the front door of the church smiling broadly

5   Matt. 15:8

and shaking hands, who earlier that morning berated his family for being slow to get in the car. It is the preacher who exhorts others to repent while himself harboring an unrepentant heart.

In each of these cases, a person uses words to indicate a relationship with God that is inaccurate. They identify with his name, but not his nature. They are those to whom Jesus asks, "Why do you call me 'Lord, Lord,' and not do what I tell you?"[6] With their speech they cry "Lord, Lord," but in their hearts they do not set him apart as such.

If it is true that out of the overflow of the heart, the mouth speaks (Luke 6:45), then the sin of lip service is not rectified by gaining control of our words. Rather, it is rectified by the cleansing of our hearts. Repentance applies the grace of Christ to our tendency to use words to cover the true state of our hearts. And that grace teaches us to say no to ungodliness (Titus 2:12). We become a people who choose silence over hypocrisy when tempted to give the appearance of godliness with our words. Sometimes the most effective means of preserving the name of the Lord from misuse is to refrain from speaking at all. At minimum, we strive consciously to keep our speech from outpacing our sanctification. We represent a holy God accurately when we preach only what we practice.

The Sin of Informality

Perhaps the most common form of misusing the name of the Lord in our time is the one I have saved for last: speaking disrespectfully of or to God by succumbing to informality.

6   Luke 6:46

One of my favorite movies is *The American President*, one of Aaron Sorkin's early contributions to helping Americans imagine what the private life of a United States president must be like. In one scene, A. J. MacInerny, the White House chief of staff, is engaged in a private discussion with President Andrew Shepherd, a man who has been his lifelong friend. Repeatedly, A. J. prefaces his comments with the words "Mr. President." At length, Shepherd admonishes him that in private he can call him by his given name: "You were the best man at my wedding, for crying out loud. Call me Andy."

To which, A. J. responds, "Whatever you say, Mr. President."

What strikes the viewer is how odd A. J.'s refusal seems at first. We live in a culture that is increasingly informal in its social practices. Clothing at work, church, and school has become more casual. Wedding invitations are less formal. Thank-you notes are now sent as emails or texts. The way we address each other has become more casual, as well. My husband doesn't call his boss "Mr. Whitmire"—he calls him Gary. Children are rarely trained to address adults as "Mr." or "Mrs." unless the adult is a teacher or a coach. We are increasingly on a first-name basis with everyone. So, when A. J. refuses to speak to his close friend by his given name, we are thrown off. Surely his personal relationship overrides his duty to the title of respect?

But A. J. recognizes the sanctity of the office of president as something that supersedes his personal relationship with the man in that office. A. J. also understands that a diminished awareness of his friend's position of authority would compromise his ability to serve the president as he should. He will not relinquish the title of respect. Or, you might say, he will not misuse the name of the president.

There is application here for the follower of Christ. It is common in Christian settings to speak of the Son of God by only his given name, Jesus:

"We're all gathered here today to worship Jesus."

"Jesus is all I need."

"Jesus changed my heart."

But interestingly, this pattern of speech is absent from the New Testament. The New Testament authors use "Jesus" to speak of the historical person, particularly when addressing unbelievers. In Acts, the speeches of Stephen, Paul, and Peter are examples of this. The Gospel writers use the name *Jesus* by itself to tell the history of the incarnation. But those who interact with him in the Gospel narratives always refer to him as "teacher" or "Lord." Only once in the Gospels does someone address him simply as "Jesus of Nazareth"—a group of demons, who in the same breath acknowledge his deity (Mark 1:24; Luke 4:34).

In all twenty-one of the Epistles, he is referred to only twenty-eight times simply as "Jesus," but 484 times by the title "Lord" or "Christ." A staggering 95 percent of the times he is mentioned, he is referred to by a title of respect.[7] But we tend to just call him Jesus. Does our frequent use of his given name indicate a lack of respect? It's certainly worth asking ourselves.

Don't miss this: a "formal" title of address is such because it is, in some sense, *formative*. By addressing others with a formal title, our conception of who they are is being formed a certain

---

7 This is my own research. I once spent an entire afternoon counting these usages and tracking them in a spreadsheet. Yes, I probably need a hobby. My counts may be off by one or two, but they're close.

way. We think differently about someone we call "Mr. President" than we do about someone we simply call "Andy." A second-grade teacher who tells her students to "just call me Susan" may find that a desire to be familiar instead of formal results in a lack of respect for her authority. Employing the formal title reinforces awareness of the respect due to its owner.

The New Testament writers take care to grant our Lord and Savior the reverence he is due. We should pay attention to this for the health of our souls. We enjoy friendship and intimacy with Christ, but we do not share equality with him. He is not our peer. Recognizing that he sits even now at the right hand of God the Father means speaking of him and to him with respect, after the pattern of the Scriptures.

Christ himself understood this when he taught us to address our prayers to the holy and kingly name of our Father in heaven. With each repetition, we reinforce our awareness of the supremacy of God and the privilege of relationship with him. Those are things I don't want to forget, and I'm prone to forgetfulness. If formal language is formative, each time we utter a formal title for the Father, the Son, or the Spirit, we practice a small liturgy that is good for our souls. And we keep the third word. We represent a transcendent God accurately when we revere his name.

Held without Guilt

"The Lord will not hold him guiltless who takes his name in vain." I would have loved if that part could have been left off the third commandment, because I am guilty. Guilty as the day is long. I am the queen of inconsistency, the maven of misattribution, the virtuoso of lip service, and the adorer of informality. And on top of that, I have been known to say a bad word or two in a moment of weakness. I am by no means guiltless. I have misused the name. I have spoken bad words.

But my guilt is removed by the blood of one who speaks a better word. When Christ Jesus proclaimed the good news of living water, the officers of the temple who were sent to arrest him marveled, saying, "No one ever spoke like this man!" (John 7:46). Nor was any deceit found in his mouth. No inconsistency of speech, no misattribution, no lip service, no low appellations. The Word made flesh kept the third word and hallowed the name. He is doing it still. We look to him as our guilt-bearer and our example. We are his people, called by his name. We pray that it would be said of us as it was said of him, "Blessed is he who comes in the name of the Lord!"[8]

On Earth as in Heaven

There is coming a day when that name will be hallowed as it should. Every knee will bow in heaven and on earth and under the earth, and every tongue will confess it.[9] It will be written on the foreheads of the faithful who surround the Lamb, who sing together:

> Who will not fear, O Lord,
>   and glorify your name?
> For you alone are holy.
>   All nations will come

8   Matt. 21:9
9   Phil. 2:10–11

and worship you,

for your righteous acts have been revealed." (Rev. 15:4)

But we need not wait until that day to respond with an expansive obedience to the third word. Indeed, we dare not, for much is at stake. It is not enough to simply refrain from profaning. We must endeavor to hallow. When we pray as we were taught, "Our Father, who art in heaven, hallowed be thy name," we repeat with the church universal and historic that the kingdom comes when its citizens confess the supremacy of their God. When God's name is hallowed on our lips and in our living, we rightly reflect him to a profane world. We shine like stars amid a crooked generation, and who knows who will be drawn to that light? There is salvation by no other name. Live as those who are marked by it. Let every other name be forgotten and this one endure. Let every other name sink into darkness and this one shine forth like the noonday sun.

Verses for Meditation

Matthew 5:33–37

Matthew 6:9

Philippians 2:9–10

Revelation 14:1

Revelation 15:4

Questions for Reflection

1. Before reading this chapter, how would you have rated your obedience to the third commandment? After reading it, how would you rate yourself? What insight accounts for the change in your diagnosis?

2. How has your understanding of the significance of the name of the Lord expanded?

3. Which of the sins of misuse of God's name are you most prone to commit (inconsistency, misattribution, lip service, or informality)? What heart issue might be driving that pattern of misuse?

4. What situations are most likely to trigger you to misuse the name of the Lord? How could you change your typical response, both your heart response and your verbal response?

Write a prayer asking God to help you to obey the third commandment. Confess where you have fallen short by using your words to defame or diminish his name. Ask him to help you speak of and to him as the Bible does. Praise him that to Christ has been given the name above all names. Thank him for calling you by his name.

4   13

The Fourth Word

Unhindered Rest

*"Remember the Sabbath day, to keep it holy. Six days you
shall labor, and do all your work, but the seventh day is
a Sabbath to the LORD your God. On it you shall not
do any work, you, or your son, or your daughter, your
male servant, or your female servant, or your livestock,
or the sojourner who is within your gates. For in six
days the LORD made heaven and earth, the sea, and all
that is in them, and rested on the seventh day. Therefore
the LORD blessed the Sabbath day and made it holy."*

EXODUS 20:8–11

IN THE OPENING LINES of the Ten Words, God prompted his
people to an act of recall: "I am the LORD your God, who
brought you out of the land of Egypt" (Ex. 20:2). He reminded
them of his mighty delivering arm just fifty days earlier. In the
fourth word, the concept of remembering is introduced again,

and this time explicitly so: "Remember the Sabbath day, to keep it holy." But this time the charge is to recall an ancient memory instead of a recent one. In the preamble to the Ten Commandments, God reminds Israel that he is her deliverer. In the fourth commandment, God reminds Israel that he is her Creator.

Instead of appealing to their recent identity as slaves, God appeals this time to their basic identity as image bearers. The practice of remembering the Sabbath requires Israel (and us) to remember what God has ordained for his children from the earliest moments of human existence: a pattern of work followed by rest, as set forth in the creation account of Genesis 1 and 2. Remember, says the fourth word, that the story of God's creative act concludes with rest. The people of God reflect him when they observe rest after labor, both by partaking of it themselves and by providing it to others.

How good is the God of Israel, who commands rest! As Israel well knew, the gods of Egypt and Canaan required labor without rest, ceaseless offerings to secure their favor. But not Yahweh. In the command to cease, God distinguishes himself from the pagan deities of Israel's past and future neighbors. In the fourth word, God answers the question, "Who is like you, O God, among the nations?" with an unequivocal "No one."

An Expansive Obedience

The Sabbath command is the longest and most detailed of the ten, and also the one most mentioned in the Old Testament. It would seem that the call to rest is one in need of emphasis and reiteration.

But how is this command to be observed today? Does it require, as it did for Israel, that a specific day in its entirety be set aside for rest? Controversy over this question has raged for centuries, and strong opinions abound. Rather than attempt to resolve the disagreement, our discussion will focus on what we can all agree upon in principle: that a good God has ordained regular rhythms of rest for those who worship him.

A bare-minimum perspective on obedience might be content to chalk out neat lines of what can and cannot be done on a certain day of the week. Such was in the heart of the Pharisee, with his requirements for how many steps might be taken or whether a grain of wheat could be plucked on the Sabbath. But the heart of the Christ-follower is drawn to an expansive obedience, asking, "How might I practice Sabbath in broader and deeper ways?"

Light in the Darkness

In 1879 the modern world changed forever with a patent. It was issued for the invention of a carbon filament made of "cotton and linen thread, wood splints, papers coiled in various ways," a process which, after fine-tuning, would launch a company the following year dedicated to commercial production of the electric light bulb.[1] The Edison Electric Company offered its customers a safer, cleaner, cheaper alternative to gaslight, and as electric power began to replace gas in homes and factories, for the first time in human history work was no longer limited to the time between sunrise and sunset. With his modern utterance of "Let there be

Holy · sanctified - set aside
focus on God Worship on God

---

1   "History of the Light Bulb: Lighting Basics," Bulbs.com, accessed July 21, 2020, https://www.bulbs.com/learning/history.aspx.

light," Thomas Alva Edison invited humanity into a world that never sleeps.

Edison himself believed sleep was a waste of time. He was known to work over one hundred hours a week, to hold job interviews at four in the morning, and to insist that his employees adhere to the same sleepless schedule he did. He adhered to and promoted a philosophy that rest was the enemy of productivity, stating in 1914 that "there is really no reason why men should go to bed at all."[2] It would appear that his vision for a sleepless humanity has come to pass, as the Centers for Disease Control and Prevention has declared a sleep deprivation epidemic among Americans.[3] Though Edison's "Let there be light" may have ushered us into sleeplessness, the divine Creator who uttered "Let there be light" also benevolently and pointedly declares "Let there be rest."

If the third word charged us to honor God with our words, the fourth charges us to honor God with our time. Just as how we use our words reveals how we view God, so does how we spend our time. Our patterns of work and rest reveal what we believe to be true about God and ourselves. God alone requires no limits on his activity. To rest is to acknowledge that we humans are limited by design. We are created for rest just as surely as we are created for labor. An inability or an unwillingness to cease from our labors is

---

2 Olga Khazan, "Thomas Edison and the Cult of Sleep Deprivation," *The Atlantic*, May 19, 2014, https://www.theatlantic.com/health/archive/2014/05/thomas-edison-and-the-cult-of-sleep-deprivation/370824/.

3 Julia Rodriguez, "CDC Declares Sleep Disorders a Public Health Epidemic," Advanced Sleep Medicine Services, Inc., December 09, 2016, https://www.sleepdr.com/the-sleep-blog/cdc-declares-sleep-disorders-a-public-health-epidemic/.

a confession of unbelief, an admission that we view ourselves as creator and sustainer of our own universes. As with Edison, this wrong thinking renders us not free, but enslaved to our ambition and enslaving of those we employ to achieve it.

We need the Sabbath command. But do we understand what it requires?

Is All Rest Sabbath Rest?

Our modern conception of Sabbath is often little more than "taking a day off" for the purpose of relaxing. But true Sabbath rest is set apart as holy: it is intended for *worship* as much as for *well-being*. The fourth word does more than tell us to relax. Sabbath rest is distinct from idleness (resting without first laboring) and different from simply having gotten enough sleep. The word *shabat* means "cease." To sabbath is to cease activity for the purpose of remembering God's provision, that we might worship him as we ought. Being well-rested and taking care of ourselves are good things, but they are at best a thin obedience to the fourth command.

More than the deliberate cessation of work for the purpose of decompressing, Sabbath is the deliberate cessation of any activity that might reinforce my belief in my own self-sufficiency. In contrast to cultural ideas of rest marked by self-care, Sabbath rest is marked by self-denial.[4] It requires that we deny ourselves the material gain or sense of accomplishment a day of labor brings. Our natural inclination is to believe that we are keeping the world

4   Mason King, "Entering God's Rest," The Village Church, September 2009, https://www.tvcresources.net/resource-library/sermons/entering-gods-rest.

rotating on its axis, a mindset that feeds a ceaseless work ethic. Sabbath presses on that mindset. It is not merely rest that restores, but rest that reorients. It reminds us that we are not God. And if we neglect it, like Edison we will most certainly drift toward the kind of work that enslaves.

Drifting from Sabbath to Slavery

At the foot of Sinai as the Ten Words were given, no one was wealthy or successful. All were recently liberated slaves learning how to live in their new freedom. What wealth they possessed had been given them as they made their hasty departure, and it was designated for the building of the tabernacle. Forty years later, when Moses would restate the Ten Words to a new generation of Israelites, he would ground the Sabbath command not in the creation story but in the Exodus story:

> You shall remember that you were a slave in the land of Egypt, and the LORD your God brought you out from there with a mighty hand and an outstretched arm. Therefore the LORD your God commanded you to keep the Sabbath day. (Deut. 5:15)

The passage of four decades would have begun the process of forgetfulness in the hearts of God's people. God knew that it would not take long for wealth-building to begin within Israel. Before long, there would be haves and have-nots. Increasingly, they would feel the pull to return to a yoke of slavery—this time, the self-appointed slavery of self-gain. So before the burden of amassing wealth besets them and the temptation of profiting off of the vulnerable presents, God gives a protective command: I, the Lord, have granted you rest from the hand of your oppressor. Don't become the oppressor yourselves.

How unthinkable, and yet, how very possible that those whose parents had known subjugation for the gain of the Pharaohs might one generation later become subjugators of others for the sake of material wealth. How unthinkable, and yet how very likely that those whose parents had been denied rest of any kind might come to deny rest for themselves and those in their care. Here we stand, these many generations hence. How much more so must we need this reminder?

Myth: Sabbath Rest Is an Individual Choice

Though all of the commands have some communal aspect, the fourth is the first one to explicitly mention others as beneficiaries of our obedience. Family, servants, animals, and anyone connected to the family of God whose labor we might be tempted to employ to secure our own rest are all protected under the Sabbath command. The connection is clear: cease your labor so others may cease theirs as well.

Here again we see that obeying the Sabbath command means self-denial: we seek to deny ourselves the ease or provision generated by the labor of others. If someone else's work secures our rest, we are more than likely enjoying the rest of privilege, but not of Sabbath. If I rest while watching someone mow my lawn or paint my toes or prepare my food, I am enjoying rest of a kind, but I may not be sabbathing. True Sabbath rest extends beyond the one resting to those who might be asked to labor on her behalf. My Sabbath rest should not create or entail labor for others in the family of God, and should be mindful of requiring work for those outside it.

Thus, community is at stake in the fourth command. There is no such thing as a noncommunal sin, and there is no such thing as a noncommunal obedience. To break a command harms more than the one who breaks it. To obey it helps both the one who obeys and the community as a whole. The command to rest recognizes this relationship. Personal sin always results in collateral damage. If the person in charge labors without rest, he denies rest to those in his charge, as well. Everyone loses. Personal obedience always results in collateral benefit. If the person in charge stops working and invites those in his charge to do so as well, everyone wins.

Thus, Sabbath observance is not just a matter of personal leisure or self-care, but of justice. It is a social leveler, an interval during which the greatest and the least enjoy the same measure of favor. Employed faithfully, it prevents exploitation. Whether employer or employee, parent or child, all partake in the gift of resting in God's provision and rediscovering our shared humanity. Those who oversee and profit from the work of others bear a special responsibility to observe Sabbath rest. By blowing the whistle for the cessation of work done on their behalf, they enable rest for all in their care.

Predict, Prepare, Partake, Provide

It follows, then, that Sabbath observance requires preparation. We begin to obey the Sabbath command *before* the Sabbath observance actually commences by arranging our lives so that work—our work and others' work—can cease for a period of time. We think about meals, chores, and other typical daily responsibilities that can be handled in advance or postponed. We consider in advance what forms of entertainment are most suitable for resetting our focus and restoring our well-being. The familiar aphorism that "if we fail to plan, we plan to fail" can be applied to observing the Sabbath. As Israel was instructed to gather a double portion of manna in preparation for the first wilderness Sabbath, we, too, can heed the principle of preparing to cease.

A lack of predictability jeopardizes Sabbath observance. By following a predictable Sabbath rhythm, we can prepare as we ought. Preparation makes it possible for us to partake of rest, and to provide it for others.

Imitating the Lord of the Sabbath

If there is joy to be found in partaking of rest, an even deeper joy is found in providing it. The Old Testament abounds with a concept of Sabbath that expands beyond the common observance of a seventh day. In the year of Jubilee, Israel was to extend its trust in God's provision by granting rest for land, rest from servitude, rest from debt (Lev. 25). Leviticus and Deuteronomy depict Sabbath as rest from suffering, for the prevention of injustice. By the time of Jesus, this broader principle had by all appearances been forgotten. But Jesus calls it to remembrance by healing a man with a withered hand on the day of ceasing:

> And he said to the man with the withered hand, "Come here." And he said to [the Pharisees], "Is it lawful on the Sabbath to do good or to do harm, to save life or to kill?" But they were silent. And he looked around at them with anger, grieved at their hardness of heart, and said to the man, "Stretch out your hand." He stretched it out, and his hand was restored. (Mark 3:3–5)

"Is it lawful on the Sabbath to do good or to do harm, to save life or to kill?" In Jesus's question and subsequent action, we hear the heart of the Sabbath command: as far as it is possible with you, grant relief to others. Remember the Sabbath.

We remember the *letter* of the Sabbath command by resting from labor.

We remember the *heart* of the Sabbath command by laboring for the rest of others.

Jesus proclaimed himself as Lord of the Sabbath. And indeed, he was. He obeyed both the letter and the heart of the Sabbath command in a literal sense. But he also obeyed in a spiritual sense. He predicted his own death, the final labor that would secure our true and better Sabbath rest. He prepared in advance for that death, laboring faithfully in obedience to the Father, and teaching his followers to walk in his steps. He partook of rest, exhaling on the cross on a Friday evening, as the sun sank to the horizon to begin the Sabbath day. And in his exhale, he breathed out rest for us—rest for our souls (Matt. 11:28–30). Jesus Christ is both the perfect practitioner of Sabbath and the means by which it is reached.

Jesus remembered the Sabbath. Those who follow him will go and do likewise.

Practical Obedience

As Jesus offered physical rest from suffering, so also we can offer rest from suffering to those God places in our path. We can take a meal to a friend who is ill. We can help watch the children of a single mom needing a break. We can tip generously those who are underpaid and rake a yard of an elderly neighbor.

Through our churches we can work collectively to alleviate the suffering of the poor in our communities and in the world. We can pay utility bills and collect diapers for teen moms and help the mentally ill to get proper counseling. We can fight human trafficking. All efforts to relieve physical suffering or bondage in the name of Jesus Christ show us to be true servants of the Lord of the Sabbath.

As Jesus offered spiritual rest for our souls, so also we can offer rest for weary souls to those God places in our path. We can proclaim with our lips the good news of Christ to those weighed down by guilt. We can proclaim with our obedient lives that true rest is found in living as loved and accepted children of God. We can intercede in prayer for the lost and the broken. We can shine like lights in the weary darkness, as beacons of Sabbath restoration and renewal. All efforts to relieve spiritual suffering or bondage in the name of Jesus Christ show us to be true servants of the Lord of the Sabbath.

On Earth as in Heaven

One day Sabbath will descend in fullness. All Sabbath now is a foretaste of Sabbath ever after. When we cease our labors and sense the sweetness of that ceasing, we anticipate the day when we will enter fully into our rest. Think about that most common of headstone inscriptions: "Rest in peace." We associate the afterlife with rest from striving. And indeed it will be that, for all who are in Christ. At the cross, Jesus justified us fully, granting us rest from the penalty of our sin. But as the author of Hebrews tells us, we still "labor . . . to enter into that rest" of freedom from the power of sin (Heb. 4:11 KJV). In other words, sanctification is actual hard work, work we will not complete until we "rest in peace" face-to-face with our Maker.

But one day, when we are glorified, we will rest fully and finally from the very presence of sin. No more futile labor to self-justify through good behavior, no more Spirit-driven labor to be holy in thought, word, and deed. The banner over the seventh day of creation is "It is finished" (Gen. 2:1–2). The banner over the believer at the cross as a new creation in Christ is "It is finished" (John 19:30). And the banner over the re-creation of all things is "It is finished" (Rev. 21:5–6). Each time we declare "It is finished" in our Sabbath observance, we affirm our allegiance to the kingdom that is to come, ordering our lives on earth as it is in heaven.

Verses for Meditation

Psalm 4:6–8

Psalm 23:1–3

Psalm 116:7–9

Matthew 11:28–30

Questions for Reflection

1. Before reading this chapter, how would you have rated your obedience to the fourth commandment? After reading it, how would you rate yourself? What insight accounts for the change in your diagnosis?

2. How has your understanding of the significance of the concept of Sabbath rest expanded?

3. Think through the Sabbath concepts of "Predict, Prepare, Partake, Provide." Which is easiest for you? Which of them needs your attention most?

4. Other than yourself, who is most impacted by your refusal to stop working and rest? How could you change your typical pattern of work/rest to better align it with one that promotes both worship and well-being?

Write a prayer asking God to help you to obey the fourth commandment. Confess where you have labored without ceasing, either physically or mentally. Ask him to help you trust his provision. Ask him to show you to whom you might grant rest in his name. Praise the Lord of the Sabbath for securing rest for your soul. Thank him for the eternal rest that is your certain future.

Delinda - Belize
Julie - Trip to Gautiamola
* Kathy Dale - Blood pressure
Oliver
Judy - Physical Therapy
Sal from Beacon - cancer - Sharon
mike strep infection
Jerilyn - Aaron & family - safety &
    bringing mom back

5

The Fifth Word

Honor Elders

*"Honor your father and your mother, that
your days may be long in the land that
the Lord your God is giving you."*

EXODUS 20:12

WE FIND OURSELVES AT the halfway point of the Decalogue, and because I am a teacher, I can't resist the temptation to give a pop quiz to make sure everyone is following along. Are you ready? We'll keep it to one question in the interest of time:

Which of the Ten Words deals with the subject of honor?

Most people would have a ready response for this question whether they had read the first four chapters of this book or not. If you were raised in a home that was even nominally Christian, it's likely a parent quoted the fifth commandment to you at one point or another to prompt you to obedience. Many a mom or dad has cited it to assure kids that their duty to their parents is written in stone by the very finger of God. To be sure, the only argument more defeating than "because I said so" is "because God said so."

The answer to my quiz seems almost too simple to justify even asking the question. The fifth word is the first and only time the word *honor* appears in the Ten Commandments. But the concept has been with us since the beginning. The first four commands exhort us to honor God rightly in thought, word, and deed. Because he is our author, he rightly holds authority over us. Our Father who art in heaven is worthy of, and entitled to, his children's honor.

The fifth word extends this exhortation from our heavenly Parent to earthly parents. Parents are our earthly "authors," and by extension, they, too exercise authority over us. The home is the lab where children learn submission to authority. Christian parents train their children to submit to them so that their children will more readily learn to submit to other earthly authorities, and ultimately, to the highest authority, our heavenly Father. A Christian parent trains her child to submit to her visible and temporary authority so that her child might one day submit to God's invisible and eternal authority.

This authority thing would all be simple if parents were perfect. But unlike our heavenly Parent, earthly parents fail and sin, disappointing and even harming their children, which can make the business of honoring them quite tricky. But more on that in a bit. We will devote some time to that reality once we have worked to understand the principle in question. The fifth word is the hinge point in the Decalogue at which the discussion of showing honoring moves from God (1–4) to human authorities (5) to one another (6–10). So, pop quiz: Which of the Ten Words deals with the subject of honor?

The answer is all of them.

The concept of honor has been with us since the first word, and it endures through the last. The Ten Commandments deal with matters of heavenly submission, earthly submission, and mutual submission—in that order. Now connect this idea to the Great Commandment, which sums up the law (Mark 12:30–31). Read it below, and mentally fill in the blank with the word that belongs there:

> You shall _____ the Lord your God with all your heart and with all your soul and with all your mind and with all your strength. . . . You shall _____ your neighbor as yourself.

Now mentally fill in the word "honor" in place of the word you just used. Read it aloud as you do. Did the meaning change? I would suggest that it only expanded. Honor is an expression of rightly ordered love. When we love as we should, we honor the object of our love as we should. It is possible to show honor whether we love an individual or not, at least outwardly. We may speak of God or others honorably while lacking love for them. We may act sacrificially toward God or others while lacking love for them. Honor rendered without love is still better for the common good than dishonor, but it is an empty obedience. Motive matters. Honor fueled by love lies at the heart of the fifth word, as it does at the heart of all ten.

Though parents may quote it to small children, the primary audience of the fifth command is adult children. It is found in the middle of a list of commands clearly addressed to adults, targeting issues that are, developmentally speaking, primarily the concerns of adulthood. Small children, though certainly sinners, do not generally carve graven images, plot murderous acts, or bear credible false witness against a neighbor.

Note the clue to the audience in the blessing that accompanies the command: longevity of life. We might paraphrase the fifth commandment as "Adult children, honor your aging parents whose days have been long upon the land, that your days might be long as well." The command bears weight on the entire length of our relationship with our parents—not just the days we lived as children in their homes. It speaks to our obligation to honor them into old age, as elaborated in Proverbs 23:22: "Listen to your father who gave you life, / and do not despise your mother when she is old."

As we noted at the outset, God's laws allow us to live in community. It is good for the community when children honor their parents by caring for them and treating them respectfully into their old age. But it is not always easy. If it were, there would only be nine commandments. Those of us who are blessed with healthy and happy relationships with our parents can still find it difficult to trade the role of cared-for for that of caregiver. Aging is, among other things, the steady progression of relinquishing one's decision-making authority. It requires deep courage, and can cause strain in even the healthiest families, as the dignity of the aging parent becomes more challenging to preserve. Under the best of circumstances, the fifth word can ask much of us.

And under hard circumstances, it can feel absolutely crushing. Those who have suffered physical, emotional, or spiritual neglect or abuse at the hands of a parent may feel at a loss as to how its requirements can (or should) be met. Here, as in all things, there is good news for those with ears to hear: "Though my father and mother forsake me, / the LORD will receive me" (Ps. 27:10 NIV).

Family of Origin, Family of Faith

The church is the family your family of origin could not be. In the Gospels, Jesus applied familial language to his followers: "Whoever does the will of my Father in heaven is my brother and sister and mother" (Matt. 12:49–50). Because of their controversial faith, first-century believers could not rely on natural family relationships. Many indeed had to leave father, mother, and brothers to follow Jesus.

The church became their spiritual family, the network of love, honor, and accountability that they needed for spiritual, emotional, and even physical support. Familial language pervades the New Testament Epistles. The Epistles address their hearers as brothers and sisters. Paul instructs Timothy to relate to younger members of his church as siblings. We will need a deep appreciation for spiritual siblinghood to navigate the remaining five commands. But for the fifth command, we must pay attention to the parent language of the New Testament. Paul instructs Timothy to relate honorably to older members as spiritual *mothers and fathers* (1 Tim. 5:1–2). He says to the church at Corinth, "For I became your father in Christ Jesus through the gospel" (1 Cor. 4:15). He even honors a spiritual mother of his own when he sends greetings to the mother of Rufus "who has been a mother to me as well" (Rom. 16:13).[1]

---

1   Portions of the following first appeared in my article, "The Church Is Not a Single-Parent Family," ChristianityToday.com, November 23, 2016, https://www.christianity today.com/ct/2016/december/church-is-not-single-parent-family.html.

This expansive application of honoring parents was not lost on earlier generations of the church. Who are we to honor in the fifth commandment? The Westminster Larger Catechism, written in 1647, responds:

> By father and mother, in the fifth commandment, are meant, not only natural parents, but all superiors in age and gifts; and especially such as, by God's ordinance, are over us in place of authority, whether in family, church, or commonwealth.[2]

Put another way, respect your elders in the broadest sense.

Note that, in alignment with the language of the Epistles and the fifth command itself, the catechism places equal emphasis on the honoring of both fathers *and* mothers. A healthy family is one in which both father and mother are valued for their wisdom and contributions. The family of God, like any healthy family, should strive to show such value to both fathers and mothers in the church. If one parenting presence is minimized or neglected, the family risks all manner of dysfunction. How beautiful is the household of God when both mothers and fathers receive the honor they are due!

Note that the catechism includes those "superior in age" under the parent umbrella. Leviticus 19:32 says, "Stand up in the presence of the aged, show respect for the elderly and revere your God. I am the Lord" (NIV). It is not just aging biological parents

---

2 Westminster Larger Catechism, Q. 124; Larger Catechism: Questions 121–130, Reformed Forum, April 21, 2008, https://reformedforum.org/podcasts/larger-catechism-questions-121-130/.

we honor, but the elderly in general. Here is a clear way to live honorably among unbelievers. In a culture that is obsessed with worshiping youth, the fifth command offers Christians a simple means to be light in the darkness.

Rather than adopt the common mantra that the elderly are adorable, irrelevant, burdensome, or expendable, we instead show them honor as full image bearers, filled with a kind of wisdom that only the passage of time can impart. By seeking out and valuing this wisdom, we honor the giver and we gain from the gift. Psalm 90:12 asks the Lord to "teach us to number our days / that we may get a heart of wisdom." How very likely that God answers this prayer through the wisdom of a saint who has numbered more days than we.

Note that the catechism further includes governing authorities under the parent umbrella, echoing Paul's admonition to give "honor to whom honor is due" (Rom. 13:7 NET). The fifth commandment reminds us that the one who holds all authority has delegated some of that authority to human rulers. By honoring those in authority over us, we fulfill the fifth command.

An Expansive Obedience

The broad application of the command grows clear: honor elders, wherever you encounter them, as far as it is possible with you. But we do so with discernment. Ephesians 6:1 helps us remember that we are to obey parents "in the Lord," or, insofar as their authority is exercised according to his will. We are not called to honor or obey elders bent on injustice or harm.

Injustice. Harm. Abuse. Abandonment. Too often, these are the practices of our elders. We rightly see them as challenges related to practical application of the fifth command, to be sure. But we must guard against seeing them as excuses. We must ask God for grace to show honor as far as it is possible with us.[3]

Maybe your mother didn't do everything right. If you're a parent yourself, you have probably learned already to extend the gracious proposition that she did the best she could. If she is living, show honor by telling her a favorite memory of her from your childhood. If you have children of your own, repeat the story to them as well. And think hard about which other stories they need to hear. Giving your children the gift of relationship with a grandparent unweighted by the baggage of your own childhood can be a way to show honor. Sometimes we honor our parents by demonstrating forgiveness in what we leave unsaid.

Maybe the father who raised you was a father in name only. Maybe he caused or allowed harm to you. Look to show honor where you can. Who acted as a father toward you? A teacher or coach? A grandfather? A pastor? A stepfather? Express your gratitude to the person or people in your life who looked beyond the boundaries of biology to demonstrate fatherly love in tangible ways. Make a donation to a cause that helps fatherless children to thrive.

Maybe your parent was the kind for whom the entire greeting card aisle was written. By all means, take your time finding the perfect card and writing the perfect sentiment on their day of honor. But also feel the weight of your privilege. To be raised by

---

3 Portions of the following are from my article "Showing Honor on Mother's Day (Even When It's Hard)," *The Beginning of Wisdom* (blog), May 8, 2013, http://jenwilkin .blogspot.com/2013/05/showing-honor-on-mothers-day-even-when.html?m=1/.

a mother or father who consistently places the needs of others above their own is no common thing. Show honor by being that kind of parent to your own children. But don't stop there. Turn your eyes to those you know who are physically, emotionally, or spiritually orphaned and be a parent to them according to their need.

Because the church is the family of God, we need be at no loss for fathers and mothers to honor. Nor need we be at a loss for spiritual orphans to parent. If your family of origin was a painful one, the family of God can be a haven and a recompense. If your family of origin was a happy one, how much more so the family of God?

In the record of the life of Jesus, we see honor given to earthly parents, the elderly, and those in authority. In the hour of his death, we see Jesus tenderly entrusting his earthly mother, Mary, into the care of his spiritual brother John. Certainly he did so out of love. But he also did so because he, of all people, understood that to honor our parents is to honor God. Because he understood his true sonship, honoring his earthly parent was a reflexive act.

The birth narrative of Jesus in the Gospel of Luke holds many memorable witnesses to his nativity. But it pointedly honors elders, as well. When Jesus is presented on the eighth day in Jerusalem, an elderly pair greets his arrival with joy. Simeon and Anna, whose days have been long upon the land, crowned with the wisdom of their white hairs, rejoice to see the Savior at last in the temple of the Lord. Their aged presence whispers a redemptive parallel to a youthful Adam and Eve cast out from the garden temple, longing for the serpent crusher to be born.

Simeon and Anna are honored fathers and mothers in the house of the Lord. And so should be all who wait expectantly on the faithfulness of God to keep his promises, even into the twilight of their years.

On Earth as in Heaven

This life is the lab in which God's children learn to submit to heavenly authority by submitting to earthly authority. Honoring our visible mothers and fathers in this life is a way of storing up treasure in heaven. By bowing to their time-tested wisdom, we prepare our hearts to bow to the timeless wisdom of God. By submitting to their visible authority, we are trained to submit our wills to the invisible authority of God. We learn by repetition, and our repeated interactions with "all superiors in age and gifts" train us for the day when at last we enter fully into the land the Lord has given us. Indeed, our days will be long upon that land. In that new creation, the one infinitely superior in age and gifts will receive the honor he is due, fully.

Today is the day to honor those-who-are-seen, that our hearts might be trained in honoring He-Who-Is-Unseen. By confessing, "Our elder, who art on earth, your name is worthy of honor," we can pray with integrity of character, "Our Father, who art in heaven, hallowed be thy name." Every failing of an earthly authority causes us to long for authority to be wielded as only God can wield it. Every honorable service of an earthly authority mirrors our Father in heaven.

Those to whom authority or seniority have been granted build the kingdom "on earth as in heaven" when they exercise that authority in wisdom and grace. Good parents make earth look and function a bit more like heaven. They bring order from chaos, a praiseworthy act to be sure. Those who are younger in wisdom or years honor God when they give honor where honor is due. Why obey the fifth command? To borrow a line from our parents, "Because God said so."

And because in doing so, we look and act like citizens of heaven.

Verses for Meditation

Leviticus 19:32
Psalm 90:12
Proverbs 23:22
Matthew 12:49–50
Ephesians 6:1–3
1 Timothy 5:1–2, 8

Questions for Reflection

1. Before reading this chapter, how would you have rated your obedience to the fifth commandment? After reading it, how would you rate yourself? What insight accounts for the change in your diagnosis?

2. How has your understanding of the importance of honoring elders expanded?

3. Which literal parent or spiritual parents could you bless this week with a word of encouragement? What virtue could you praise them for? What past action or word could you thank them for? What shortcoming might you forgive them for in your heart?

4. Who has the Lord placed in your life for you to parent, either literally or spiritually? What shortcomings make you feel inadequate or unworthy of honor? How can you best employ your experience and godly wisdom to their benefit?

Write a prayer asking God to help you to obey the fifth commandment. Confess where you have fallen short by avoiding or forgetting to show honor to elders. Ask him to bring to mind specific people to honor and specific ways to do so. Praise him for being the perfect parent and for providing the family of God for you through Christ. Thank him for calling you his child.

6

The Sixth Word

Honor Life

"You shall not murder."

EXODUS 20:13

IMAGES HOLD GREAT POWER to move us. Our reaction to an image is driven by the way we feel about the person or idea it represents. From stained glass to monuments to insignias on flags, we respond viscerally depending on the underlying association. If you've ever saved a photo of a deceased loved one or cropped someone out of a photo in sadness or hurt, you reveal your understanding of the connection between the image and the person it represents. The last six commandments will press us to evaluate how we respond to the image of God as represented in our fellow man. They will warn us that all mistreatment of our image-bearing neighbor springs from an underlying desire to denigrate God himself. And they will exhort us that love of our image-bearing neighbor must spring from love of God.

At Least I Haven't Done That

In 2004, I was the mother of four children ranging in age from eight to four. Reality TV was itself a small child, with *Survivor* entering into its fourth season. But 2004 would be the year that parents of small children received a gift from the reality TV gods in the form of a show called *Supernanny*. "Outwit, Outplay, Outlast" had proven a winning formula on *Survivor*, and as someone attempting to survive another overwhelming set of circumstances, I was drawn to its parallel themes in a show about parenting.

So were six million other people. *Supernanny* exploded in popularity in its first year as parents everywhere tuned in to watch Jo Frost sort out the mayhem in other parents' homes. *Supernanny* rapidly spread to forty-eight different countries, becoming one of the biggest success stories in reality TV.[1] I am not an expert in what drives ratings, but in this case, I have a thought. Well, not so much a thought as a confession: I did not watch *Supernanny* to get parenting help. I watched it for validation. And I suspect I was not alone.

Seeing other parents with far bigger issues than I had gave me the opportunity to tell myself I wasn't such a terrible parent after all. Yes, I had lost my temper, and yes, my house was a disaster, but these other parents needed Supernanny to sweep in and walk them through the most elementary parenting dilemmas. Rather than turning off the TV and thinking, "Well, tomorrow I will try that," I thought, "Well, at least I haven't done that."

---

1 Sean Macaulay, "Jo Frost Interview," *The Telegraph*, January 28, 2010, https://www.telegraph.co.uk/culture/7051886/Jo-Frost-interview.html.

I suspect this is why reality shows about murders are so popular. Whatever else they may stir in us, they help us lay our heads on our pillows reminded that, whatever we may be, we are *not-murderers*.

The Ten Words, by their very nature, are not validating statements. They do not boost our confidence that we are doing just fine. But the sixth word, taken by itself, can sometimes be heard that way. It can feel like a reprieve in the middle of a courtroom trial, a moment to draw a breath of relief and say, "Well, at least I haven't done that." If asked to point to one of the Ten Commandments we can say with confidence we have never broken, most of us would respond with this one. But I think we would be served to look for help of a better kind from its words.

And its words are noticeably few. If we were reading the Ten Words aloud from start to finish, the sixth is where the pace changes noticeably. No promise or warning is attached, no editorializing of any kind, just a short utterance: "You shall not murder." Terse and succinct, the sixth word uses only two Hebrew words to make its point.

When a point is obvious, it requires fewer words to make. On the surface, the danger the command highlights appears both obvious and easily avoidable. What could be more straightforward than being a *not-murderer*? But we should not infer that just because the sixth word is brief, it is easy to understand or simple to obey. The Pharisees of Jesus's day seem to have made that mistake, as we will see.

It is not just the pace that changes with the sixth word, but the focus. Having given five exhortations to honor God and elders, the Ten Words now turn their attention to the business of honoring one another as fellow image bearers. We progress from discussion of how we relate to our heavenly Parent, to our earthly parents (human authorities), to our brothers and sisters (our neighbors). Essentially, the last five words will speak to the proper treatment of siblings.[2] If you grew up with a natural sibling, you can no doubt guess why these commands are needed.

Siblings and Image Bearers

Supernanny had a few things to say about sibling rivalry. That's no surprise, as it is one of the earliest manifestations of sin in human history. As soon as the first parents produced a pair of siblings, it ensued. The story of Cain and Abel could not be more tragic. Not long after Adam and Eve are cast from the garden, clinging to the promise of a deliverer, Eve gives birth to Cain. She rejoices that she has "gotten a man with the help of the LORD" (Gen 4:1). Jim Boice notes that her reaction points back to the promise she had received, that *through her male offspring* the serpent would be crushed (Gen. 3:15). She says, in effect, "Here he is!" Though you and I know the wait for Messiah will be millennia, Eve would not have.[3]

The reader feels the weight of the irony. For Cain is not Messiah but murderer—the firstborn of Adam will be the first to take the life of a sibling made in the image of God (Gen. 9:6). Seeing that his brother Abel has received God's favor, he is enraged. God warns

2 The Ten Commandments are typically separated into two tables to reflect which ones address love of God and which ones address love of neighbor. Here, I am not making a statement about where to divide the two tables. I am simply noting the way authority shapes our understanding of the first five versus the last five.

3 James Montgomery Boice, *Genesis: An Expositional Commentary*, Vol. 1, *Creation and Fall (Genesis 1–11)* (Grand Rapids, MI: Baker, 2006), 250–51.

him: "Why are you furious? And why do you look despondent? If you do what is right, won't you be accepted? But if you do not do what is right, sin is crouching at the door. Its desire is for you, but you must rule over it" (Gen. 4:6–7 CSB).

Cain does not heed the warning, or master the temptation. He cannot strike down God, so he strikes down the one who resembles him. He lures Abel into a field and slays him. When God inquires about his victim, Cain demurs with a scathing inquiry of his own: "Am I my brother's keeper?" (Gen. 4:9). It is the question all of us must ask and answer, every day of our lives, and it is the question that our five remaining commands answer pointedly.

But what can we learn from this earliest episode of murder? Are we to regard Cain through narrow eyes and tell ourselves, "Well at least I haven't done that"? If we look carefully, we find that his path to becoming a murderer did not start with plotting murder. It began with a far more ubiquitous sin. It began with being angry.

But is anger a sin? Anger is a negative emotion, like fear or sorrow. An emotion is a natural response to a circumstance. In particular, anger is our natural response to the violation of our wills. If all anger were sinful, we would not need the reminder, "Be angry and do not sin" (Eph. 4:26). Instead, the verse would simply read, "Do not get angry." There is such a thing as righteous anger—anger whose aim is to defend God's holiness, with no thought for self. Jesus demonstrates this in the Gospels. But if we are honest, we can acknowledge that we rarely feel that sort of anger without at least a hint of self-righteousness mixed in to contaminate it.

Both positive and negative emotions are a gift from God, not sinful in and of themselves. But they can quickly progress to being sinful if we do not manage them properly. Genesis 4 does not say that Cain's anger was sinful, but we can guess that it was because of where it led him. Cain's problem was not mere anger, but anger nursed, anger indulged, anger gratified.

We can also guess that his anger was sinful because of Jesus's words about the sixth word. By the time of his earthly ministry, the Pharisees had become experts in the art of "At least I haven't done that." Jesus even tells a parable about a Pharisee and a tax collector to illustrate this particular brand of legalism.[4] The Pharisees were content that they had fulfilled all that the law required as long as they had obeyed it outwardly. Like a child taking just enough bites of dinner to merit dessert, they were content to let the letter of the law limit their obedience to a bare minimum outward show of compliance, no matter the state of their hearts. In the case of the sixth command, they, like us, were happy to mark its requirement as fulfilled because they were *not-murderers* in the most literal sense.

An Expansive Obedience

In the Sermon on the Mount, Jesus responds to this stinginess of spirit by pressing his hearers toward an expansive obedience to several Old Testament commands, starting with the sixth word in particular:

> You have heard that it was said to those of old, "You shall not murder; and whoever murders will be liable to judgment." But I say to you that everyone who is angry with his brother will be

4 Luke 18:9–14

liable to judgment; whoever insults his brother will be liable to the council; and whoever says, "You fool!" will be liable to the hell of fire. (Matt. 5:21–22)

Jesus does not overturn the command not to murder. Rather, he challenges our affection for bare-minimum compliance. A bare-minimum approach to "You shall not murder" means I believe that as long as I don't commit the physical act of murder, I have fulfilled the law. But Jesus teaches the better way. He urges his hearers to look beyond the letter of the law to the spirit of the law. He takes great care to help his hearers identify the inward sin that accounts for why murder happens in the first place. And by pointing to anger as its origin, he allows no room for any of us to breeze past the sixth word.

Just as God warned Cain that his anger was leading somewhere brutal, Jesus warns us. He does so by describing speech patterns that result from anger indulged. When we come to the ninth word, we will more deeply consider how our use of words relates to our emotions, but for now, we can examine the progression of sin Jesus presents: a negative emotion can lead to harmful thinking, to harmful speech, and to harmful actions.

The exclamation "You fool" is the Hebrew word *raca*, the ancient equivalent of our most defamatory language, the kind that requires bleeping out. It is a term of extreme contempt. The movement from anger to insult to "Raca!" might be mapped like this: First, I am angry with you in response to a hurt. Next, I begin to question your character with an insult. Then, I begin to question your worth as a person. As anger degrades into contempt, the personhood of another is devalued. Dallas Willard notes:

[Contempt] is a kind of studied degradation of another, and it also is more pervasive in life than anger. It is never justifiable or good. . . . In contempt, I don't care if you are hurt or not. Or at least so I say. You are not worth consideration one way or another. We can be angry at someone without denying their worth. But contempt makes it easier for us to hurt them or see them further degraded. . . . The intent and effect of contempt is always to exclude someone, push them away, leave them isolated.[5]

People who murder have embraced contempt to the point that they believe another image bearer to be so worthless as to not deserve to live. People who embrace contempt have indulged anger to the point that they believe their injury merits the greater injury of another. People who indulge anger have made a conscious decision of the will to nurture a negative emotion into a viable seedling of contempt, a seedling which, over time, yields a bloody harvest.

Is Jesus adding to the law by broadening our attention from murder to anger and contempt? By no means. He is pointing out the seedling that grows into the thorny vine that chokes out life. He is appealing to us to fastidiously weed the garden of personal holiness. He is teaching that if every person dealt with anger quickly and rightly, there would be no need for the sixth word at all.

The impulse to murder is nothing less than the outer workings of a lesser impulse we choose to indulge on a regular basis. From

5   Dallas Willard, *The Divine Conspiracy: Rediscovering Our Hidden Life in God* (San Francisco: HarperSanFrancisco, 1998), 151–52.

Little League games to rush-hour traffic jams, we see evidence around us that people regularly express anger beyond what a circumstance merits. We indulge and overexpress it routinely. Our exaggerated responses reveal that we did not simply become angry in the instance, but that we carry a supply of pent-up anger with us at all times.[6]

Shrewd observers have figured out how to profit from our anger-hoarding. A recent article in *The Atlantic* calls these profiteers "anger merchants": daytime talk shows airing brawls to the delight of viewers, cable news networks fueling moral indignation, social media platforms happily rewarding vented anger with likes and shares. Our politicians forgo civility for outrage, and we choose a side and join in the carnival of contempt.[7] Us versus them. We are the righteous, and they? They are not merely the unrighteous; they are worthless.

Allow me a simple illustration from my own life. If I am walking into my home and see a ladybug on my doorstep, I smile and take care to relocate it to the nearest plant. But if I see a cockroach, I have a different response. Why? Because I feel affection for one and contempt for the other. Any decent entomologist would tell me that these two creatures are essentially equals, but I have devoted myself to elevating one to "delightful" and the other to "despicable." A faulty entomology has its consequences, but how much more so a faulty anthropology? Contempt directed at an image bearer breeds all manner of violence.

6   Willard, *Divine Conspiracy*, 149.
7   Charles Duhigg, "The Real Roots of American Rage," *The Atlantic*, July 15, 2019, https://www.theatlantic.com/magazine/archive/2019/01/charles-duhigg-american-anger/576424/.

Contempt may win followers, but it is not pastoral. It masquerades as righteous anger, but it is, in fact, self-serving and self-elevating. It may make a point, but it always has a victim. We may deflect our connection to its victims by asking, "Am I my brother's keeper?" but the blood-bought children of God know the answer to our own question. Because Christ, our brother, has answered it fully and finally with his "yes."

He himself, the object of anger and contempt, denigrated and devalued, and stripped of his dignity, endured the breaking of the sixth word in his broken flesh and spilled blood. Cain the murderer was not Messiah. Christ the murdered is Messiah indeed. Because he is the image of the invisible God, those who hated God dealt violently with that image. Yet he whose life was extinguished took every care to preserve life. And in receiving back his own, he lives that we may have life.

On Earth as in Heaven

We are dearly loved children because of Christ's life-giving act. In him was life. Who then, being found in him, can be an instrument of death? Because we are accepted in the beloved, we will not be content to simply be *not-murderers*, or *not-contemptuous*, or *not-angry*. We will not merely refrain from taking life—we will run toward giving it. Let us read in the sixth word's prohibition of murder the exhortation to take every care to preserve life. Let us run to be *life-protectors* and *esteem-givers* and *peacemakers*.

To do so will require that we take stock of how we might be participating in the anger-worship of our cultural moment. It will require that we strive to preserve life in a culture that believes entire categories of image bearers are worthy of our contempt or our disregard—the unborn, the elderly, the physically or mentally challenged, the poor, the powerless, the foreigner. And in a world defined by living at odds with others, it will require that we strive to live at peace with others, as far as it is possible with us. It will ask us to be our brothers' keepers, even as Christ has been ours.

When we live in this way, motivated to preserve and promote life as the joyful recipients of eternal life, our spheres of influence become outposts of the kingdom of heaven on earth, microcosms of that glorious city whose very center is a tree of life. In that city, anger and contempt are no more, and those who bear the image of Christ are honored by one another in thought, word, and deed. The old has passed away, been laid to rest, been crucified with Christ. When we are slow to become angry and quick to forgive, when we root out the thorny vine of bitterness from the garden of our personal holiness, we honor the sixth word and affirm our allegiance to the kingdom that is to come, ordering our lives on earth as it is in heaven.

Verses for Meditation

Genesis 4:1–12
Genesis 9:6
Romans 12:14–20
Romans 13:9
1 John 3:11–12

Questions for Reflection

1. Before reading this chapter, how would you have rated your obedience to the sixth commandment? After reading it, how

would you rate yourself? What insight accounts for the change in your diagnosis?

2. How has your understanding of the significance of the command not to murder expanded?

3. How prevalent is anger in your life? At whom is it most often directed? How might you be indulging that anger in a way that tempts you to devalue the person who triggers it?

4. What is your typical response to the person who angers you most, both your heart response and your verbal response? What life-giving response could you have instead the next time he or she makes you angry?

Write a prayer asking God to help you to obey the sixth commandment. Confess where you have fallen short by indulging anger and contempt in your heart or in your relationships. Ask him to help you react to the offenses of others with forgiveness and reconciliation. Thank him for Christ our brother, who is indeed our keeper.

7

The Seventh Word

Honor Marriage

"You shall not commit adultery."

EXODUS 20:14

IF YOU ARE UNMARRIED, resist the urge to skip this chapter. The most famous unmarried man in all of history had much to say about marriage, so perhaps you will find help here. If you are married and have not committed adultery, and have no plans to do so, keep reading, as well. We have come to the seventh word, as brief as the sixth, and, as we will see, equally as expansive in application. Once again, Jesus will teach us that there is a deeper obedience to be sought, one that surpasses simply not sleeping with someone we are not married to. Once again, we must ask what our treatment of someone who bears the image of God indicates about our hearts.

It will be necessary to talk about self-mutilation before we are done, so keep a sharp pair of scissors handy, and read on.

I'm kidding about the scissors.

God takes the marriage covenant seriously. Genesis 2:24 describes marriage as the joining of a man and a woman into one flesh. It is a word picture to illustrate both the permanence and the interconnectedness of the marriage relationship. The seventh word forbids adultery as the blatant dismantling of what God has joined. In the Old Testament it was punishable by death (Lev. 20:10). In the New Testament it is stated as clear grounds for divorce (Matt. 5:32). It is the consistent metaphor used to describe the unfaithfulness of the people of God.

The seventh word tells us to take marriage and sexual purity as seriously as God does. The word *adulterate* means "to corrupt, debase, or make impure."[1] Unfaithfulness in marriage corrupts the purity of the union, debasing what God has declared holy. Because all personal sin yields collateral damage, adultery also corrupts and debases the stability of the family unit and the community. Marital dysfunction causes a ripple effect, harming more than just the adulterer.

Seen in the positive, the seventh word shows us how to love one another through healthy marriages. Just as the command against murder asked us to be life protectors, the command against adultery asks us to be marriage honorers. Faithful, healthy marriages are not good just for the family; they are good for the community. Marriage is the foundational relationship in the home from which all others proceed, and to which all others look for identity and stability. Functional marriages tend to build functional homes that require less intervention from the community. Often, these

---

1   *Merriam-Webster*, s.v. "adulterate," accessed July 21, 2020, https://www.merriam-webster.com/dictionary/adulterate/.

homes are capable of giving more than they take, thereby helping the community thrive as a whole.

We saw with the sixth word that anger and contempt created the ecosystem for murder by devaluing another image bearer. Adultery is addressed after murder (rather than before) because it, too, is an outward sinful act that begins with the devaluing of another. Anger and contempt toward a spouse create the ecosystem for adultery by devaluing both the spouse and the marriage union: I thought at the altar that you were worthy of my love and commitment. I see now that you are not as valuable as I had thought. You are a disappointment. You stir *raca* in my throat. I will direct my attention elsewhere.

And the nature of my attention will not be (as it so often is portrayed in romantic comedies) a search for a soul mate. It will instead be a search for the gratification of a particular expression of contempt, one that underlies the adulterous act: lust. Furthermore, it will not be "stumbled into" by someone swept away by passion. No, rather it will be *committed*, willed, perpetrated. As he did with the sin of murder, Jesus points us to the root of the sin of adultery in the Sermon on the Mount:

> You have heard that it was said, "You shall not commit adultery." But I say to you that everyone who looks at a woman with lustful intent has already committed adultery with her in his heart. (Matt. 5:27–28)

Lust lies at the root of adultery. Thus, the seventh word speaks to more than just those of us who are married, but to all who are tempted to lust. Just as we would avoid murder altogether if we dealt with our temptation to feed our anger, we would avoid sexual impurity altogether if we dealt with our temptation to lust. We examined how prevalent anger is in our culture, and how it has been monetized and weaponized. So also has lust been culturally normalized and appropriated to suit the ends of those who would profit from it. It saturates our media, selling us a bent version of human flourishing that is based on debasing the good gifts of sex and sexuality.

Lust itself is an act of contempt, reducing someone to a source of sexual gratification and nothing more. If the sixth command prohibited regarding our neighbor as *expendable*, the seventh prohibits regarding our neighbor as *consumable*.

Note that Jesus condemns "everyone who looks at a woman with lustful intent." Lust takes many forms, but the specific form linked to adultery is what 1 John 2:16 refers to as the "lust of the eyes" (NIV)—desire that is stirred and strengthened by seeing. This is not a casual glance, in which we may notice that another person is attractive. Rather, it is the lingering look, the evaluating gaze. It is the meditative *seeing* that leads to objectified *desiring* that ends in self-justified *consuming* of that which is off limits. And it is as old as the garden.

It is Eve gazing at forbidden fruit, finding it desirable, and consuming it. What Jesus identifies as the root of adultery is the very thing that lies at the root of every adulterated act. The lust of the eyes is a disordered desire, one that chooses to fix its gaze, its yearning, and its grasp on that which God has forbidden.[2]

2　The concept of disordered desires, or "loves," comes to us from the fourth-century theologian Augustine of Hippo. His book, *Confessions*, explores the idea at length.

Though lust of the eyes can apply generally, in the context of the seventh word it applies specifically to disordered sexual desire. Disordered desires result in disordered lives. The resulting sin of adultery is bad not just for the couple, but for the community.

Jesus points his teaching at husbands, likely because in the culture of his day the cost for adultery hit women much harder than men. It meant catastrophic social and financial ruin, and, as in the case of the woman caught in adultery, it could even mean death.[3] It is revealing that her story does not depict even a whiff of outrage directed at the man caught in adultery with her, though he must certainly have been nearby. As in Jesus's day, the lust of the eyes exacts a high cost from women. Of the millions of image bearers currently trafficked for sex, 98 percent are women and girls.[4]

Nevertheless, we must be clear that the lust of the eyes is no respecter of sex or marital status. It besets both Adams and Eves. Later in the Sermon on the Mount, Jesus will note that the eye is the lamp of the body, the portal through which we are filled either with light or with darkness (Matt. 6:22). We have eyes aplenty, both men and women. Thus, we all have opportunity to sin with them. Or to gouge them out. But let's leave that part for a minute longer.

Desire Disordered

Sexual desire inside the marriage covenant is an expression of mutual love. It is a rightly ordered desire. Sexual desire outside

3   John 8:1–11
4   "Bought and Sold, The Sex Trafficking of Women & Girls," LiveYourdream.org, accessed July 21, 2020, https://www.liveyourdream.org/media/action-resources /Trafficking/sex-trafficking-facts-infographic.pdf.

of marriage is an expression of lust. It is a disordered desire. Sex inside of marriage is about commitment and vulnerability, the letting down of our guard and the literal joining of two fleshes into one. Sex outside of marriage is about consumption and vulgarity, the acquisition of pleasure in the short term, the thin appearance of love, the joining of what God has not joined. Sexual lust is many unsavory things, but it is certainly the temptation to avoid vulnerability and commitment.

How else would pornography establish such a foothold, unless it promised the gratification of desire without vulnerability or commitment? It enters through the lamp of the body, filling it with darkness, whispering the very same lie that Eve believed in her seeing: "It won't hurt to look." Promiscuity, marketed to us in movies and sitcoms, holds forth a more socially acceptable feast for the eyes, but it is doing much the same thing to our spiritual vision as porn—normalizing disorder, glamorizing sex without commitment. But of course, porn goes further, abandoning any pretense of consensual union and celebrating degradation of another.

Whether the lust of the eyes indulges itself at the community pool or on a screen, those who gaze must convince themselves that the person they are viewing deserves, or even wants, to be consumed. We do not consume those we love; we treasure and protect them as image bearers. Thus, the root sin of adultery chooses a person it is willing to treat with contempt. Lust devalues its object, so that the act of adultery becomes the next logical step. As he did with murder and anger, Jesus does not equate adultery with lust. He shows how one results from the other, a rancid seed yielding rotten fruit. And he warns us to root it out.

The apostle Paul does, as well. Certainly lust is the norm in our hypersexualized culture, but it has also found ways to be normalized within the church. Too often it is seen as a beast to be tamed. Yet, Paul seemed to think differently on the matter of sexual immorality. He seemed to think we could kill it: "Put to death therefore what is earthly in you: sexual immorality, impurity, passion, evil desire, and covetousness, which is idolatry" (Col. 3:5).

Satan has succeeded in convincing believers that lust is just something to be managed instead of something to be slain. God intends for us to strike it down. But what is the knife that slays the beast? *Word of God.*

I promised you dismemberment, and I won't disappoint. Immediately after Jesus connects adultery to the lust of the eyes, he makes this startling statement:

> If your right eye causes you to sin, tear it out and throw it away. For it is better that you lose one of your members than that your whole body be thrown into hell. And if your right hand causes you to sin, cut it off and throw it away. For it is better that you lose one of your members than that your whole body go into hell. (Matt. 5:29–30)

If ever a passage tested those who hold to a literal reading of Scripture, it is this one. Is Jesus actually suggesting that the solution to lust is self-mutilation? The church father Origen believed so, and backed up his belief by emasculating himself. The church rightfully denounced such actions, for what at first appears to be an effective, albeit, dramatic solution does not solve the problem at all. Dallas Willard notes:

Of course being acceptable to God is so important that, if cutting bodily parts off could achieve it, one would be wise to cut them off. . . . But so far from suggesting that any advantage could be gained in this way, Jesus' teaching in this passage is exactly the opposite. . . . The deeper question always concerns who you are, not what you did or can do. . . . If you dismember your body to the point where you could never murder or even look hatefully at another, never commit adultery or even look to lust, your *heart* could still be full of anger, contempt, and obsessive desire for what is wrong, no matter how thoroughly stifled or suppressed it may be.[5]

If only the conquering of lust were as simple as removing the offending member. But as with all sin, our offending eyes and hands and feet and ears and lips and tongues and noses serve at the pleasure of our hearts. What our hearts delight to do, our members rush to accomplish. We need a better blade than any forged by human hands, one aimed at ridding our hearts of disordered desires.

Praise God, we have one. The blade that slays the beast is the word of God, made living and active by the Spirit of God, dividing thoughts and intentions of the heart (Heb. 4:12). By the word of God we learn to delight our hearts in the Lord, and the outcome is that which the psalmist predicts: "Delight yourself in the LORD, / and he will give you the desires of your heart" (Ps. 37:4).

As we confess and repent, God puts to death our disordered desires and gives us rightly ordered ones. And our eyes and hands

---

5   Dallas Willard, *The Divine Conspiracy: Rediscovering Our Hidden Life in God* (San Francisco: HarperSanFrancisco, 1998), 167–68.

and feet and ears and lips and tongues and noses begin to serve at the pleasure of a heart that delights in him.

An Expansive Obedience

"If your eye is healthy, your whole body will be full of light" (Matt. 6:22). The antidote to the lust of the eyes is not self-inflicted blindness, but seeing as God sees. Though humans look at the outside, God looks at the inside. We must see ourselves rightly, but we must also see our neighbor rightly, unclouded by disordered desire. If we were to look at one another with the lingering gaze that sees what God sees, what would we behold?

In the world around us, we would see fellow humans created in the image of God, in desperate need of a sustained gaze from us that restores their dignity rather than robs it—the sort of gaze with which Jesus looked upon those like the woman with an alabaster jar, who had only known the lingering gaze of lust and its consequences. He gave her back what others had taken: full humanity.

Within the church, the family of God, we would see *adelphoi*, brothers and sisters. Here, too, we are in desperate need of offering the sustained gaze of nonsexualized relational trust, such as a brother gives to a dearly loved sister. Instead of potential sex partners to be consumed, we would see precious siblings to be cherished. The church has devoted much energy to separating men from women to prevent impropriety. But this is effectively eye-gouging instead of seeing as God sees. We cannot edify and encourage one another, or even properly value one another, if we are perpetually kept apart.

To those who are single, when sexual desire announces itself in a relationship, ask yourself what lies at its root. Is it a response to seeing the inner person, or is it a response of a different kind, set on consuming?

To those who are married, remember that noticing someone else is normal. Lingering on that notice is not. As he who called you is faithful, you also be faithful.

To both single and married followers of Christ, keep your eye healthy. It hurts to look. But remember never to police your eye or your hand to the neglect of your heart. By all means, don't commit acts that spring from lust. But put to death lust, not merely its fruit.

We should not commit adultery. We should not indulge lust. But what *should* we do? We should restore dignity to those who have suffered at the hands of a culture steeped in the lie that "It won't hurt to look." Those committed to keeping the seventh word become their sister's keeper, working to end sex trafficking and rehabilitate those it has exploited. They advocate for victims of sexual abuse. They work to raise a generation of sons and daughters who understand pornography as lethal, not just to the individual or to marriages, but to the community. They fight against messages and images that objectify women and men. And they embrace and model sexual fidelity.

On Earth as in Heaven

Too many believers have absorbed the cultural message that lust is our lot from here to the grave. But Christ has inaugurated a better kingdom among us. To all whose right hands offend, our Lord proclaims the kingdom of heaven is at hand. By the power of the Spirit we apply ourselves daily to say no to ungodliness, putting to death sexual immorality and the lingering gaze that invites it. We gain access to this better kingdom by his blood, and we inhabit it by fixing our gaze on him.

The lust of the eyes is the inverse of the desire we were created to express. We were created to desire holiness—to fix our eyes on it, and to meditate on it, and to feast on it. Adam and Eve fixed their eyes on what was forbidden, and the old creation was adulterated. We, as new creations in Christ, fix our eyes on him from whence comes our help.

Delight yourself in lawlessness, and your disordered desires will govern you. Delight yourself in the Lord, and he will give you new desires. Make his law your delight, and meditate on it day and night. In doing so, you practice the meditative *seeing* that leads to holy *desiring*, that ends in the consecrated *consuming* of the very bread of life. The result of that feast is a right eye that honors others and a right hand that works to give them dignity. Such eyes and hands make manifest the kingdom here and now.

One day he shall return, and every eye that has desired to consume its neighbor shall rest its gaze on the desire of nations. Every adulterated act shall cease. No longer will anyone objectify or exploit his neighbor. The family of God will stand with eyes filled with health and hearts filled with light. The final faithful marriage of which all others have been a whisper will take place in purity and power. The mouth of the Lord has spoken it. The zeal of the Lord Almighty shall accomplish it. Until that day, in every act of delighting in the Lord, we express our eagerness for that great marriage covenant to be sealed. "The Spirit and the Bride say, 'Come.' And let the one who hears say, 'Come.'"

Verses for Meditation

Psalm 37:4

Proverbs 6:32

Matthew 5:27–30

Matthew 6:22–23

Colossians 3:5–6

Hebrews 13:4

Questions for Reflection

1. Before reading this chapter, how would you have rated your obedience to the seventh commandment? After reading it, how would you rate yourself? What insight accounts for the change in your diagnosis?

2. How has your understanding of the significance of the concept of lust expanded? Specifically, how does the lust of the eyes figure into your own sin patterns? In what situations are you most likely to believe the lie that "It won't hurt to look"?

3. To what extent have you embraced the cultural lie that lust is something to be tamed rather than put to death? If you believe that the sharp blade of the Scriptures can put it to death and reshape your desires, what regular practice of gazing on them do you follow?

4. In response to this chapter, what tangible action should you take? What should you stop doing? What should you start doing? What does an expansive obedience to the seventh word ask of you, specifically?

Write a prayer asking God to help you to obey the seventh word. Confess where you have participated in our culture's lust addiction. Ask him to help you have right eyes for those exploited and degraded by it, and right hands to help them. Ask him to give you a healthy view of sexual desire and its role in your life. Praise him that, in Christ, we receive new desires. Thank him for sending a faithful bridegroom to his people.

8

The Eighth Word

Honor Property

"You shall not steal."
EXODUS 20:15

I HAVE TWO CLEAR MEMORIES of committing theft before the age of three and a half. I know what my age was because we moved to Texas the summer after my third birthday, and the memories are definitely from Alabama. The first act of thievery occurred at the local hardware store, where I pilfered a small ceramic hook from a bin placed at my eye level. It was shaped like a swan. So, obviously, I took it. The second act occurred at the next-door neighbor's house. I helped myself to a bracelet, the kind made of elastic and plastic jewels that usually comes in a set with a tiara and a ring. One does not conceal such a piece of glam, and thus, my mother noticed it on my skinny wrist and promptly ordered me to return it. She had also spotted the swan before we made it to the parking lot.

Here is the moral of my story: if you're going to steal, be better at it than I was.

No, the moral of my story is that we determine at a young age that ill-gotten gain is gain, nonetheless. The lure of stealing is that we might gain "something for nothing." But all stealing is gain at someone else's unwilling expense, whether that expense is small or large. Stealing, like murder and adultery, is an expression of contempt, answering wrongly the question, "Am I my brother's keeper?"

Why We Steal

Perhaps the most notable example of contempt-fueled theft in Scripture is the story of Jacob's two-fold robbery of his brother Esau. Jacob uses deception to steal both the birthright and the blessing from Esau. He believes himself cleverer than both his brother and his father. What is most ironic (and perhaps most instructive) from this tale is that he steals two things that God had already promised would belong to him, before he was even born. It's the equivalent of someone embezzling from a family business he stands to inherit. Clever indeed.

Jacob steals what God had already ordained would be his. If you're going to steal, be better at it than he was.

Better yet, just obey the eighth word. Jacob's story has much to say to us as we consider its familiar cadence: "You shall not steal." As soon as we hear it, we recall times when we have done it, times when we have contemplated it, and times when we have judged others for doing it. Indeed, we judge Jacob every year when our Bible reading plans whisk us through Genesis. You probably judged me when you read the first paragraph of this chapter. The thing with stealing is that we can always find someone else who is doing it on a grander scale than we are. Sometimes that grander scale measures the thief's ineptitude, like a car thief who posts his joyride to social media. Sometimes that grander scale measures the thief's skill, like the CFO whose embezzlement scheme hits the national news.

What we need most from these stories is the reassurance that, whatever our sticky-fingered sins, they don't come close to "real stealing."

And by "real stealing," we usually mean the kind that can get you arrested, or fired, or both. Every civilized society recognizes stealing as a crime. Laws to prohibit it protect our rights to own private property, whether intellectual or physical. For Israel, fresh out of slavery and few in personal belongings, the eighth word set a clear expectation that theirs was to be a civilized society, as well. The longer God prospered them, the more issues of personal ownership would affect the community.

Thus, God takes immediate action to move them from the idea that stealing is "something for nothing" to the idea that crime doesn't pay. Though the eighth commandment is few in words, its application is expounded in the Book of the Covenant, the three chapters immediately following the Decalogue in Exodus 20–23. There we find considerable discussion of what is not to be stolen, how thieves are to be punished, and what level of restitution must be made to ensure that thievery yields great loss instead of profit. Stealing "helps" the individual at the expense of the community. The act itself is an expense, but so also is the work it takes to rectify the act. Every year millions of dollars are spent to prevent or prosecute various forms of theft in the United States alone. Stealing multiplies injury to the common good.

And as with murder and adultery, stealing is an expression of contempt. If I can steal from someone, I'm probably not going to pray for her or seek her good. Stealing prays, "My kingdom come, my will be done." It turns to my neighbor and demands, "Give me this day my daily bread."

What We Steal

Christians steal. Against all logic, we steal like everyone else, seeking to gain at someone else's expense. If only we could learn from Jacob's story that God has already given us birthright and blessing in Christ. Innumerable riches. In him we have an imperishable inheritance that is kept in heaven for us. But heaven is annoyingly invisible, so we turn to the visible and find that we would just as soon store up treasure here.

We may succeed in avoiding the more sociopathic forms of stealing, only to fail in avoiding the more socially acceptable ones. You know the ones I mean, the ones everybody does. I speak as a person who routinely pulls dozens of pens out of the bottom of my bag, none of which I purchased, nor do I even remember taking. Please don't tell my mom.

These are the kinds of stealing that we wink at or give no thought to, scarcely even identifying them as sinful. They are the ones we can most easily convince ourselves are of no harm to anyone, so why not? What sets them apart is that we believe them to be victimless. One of the most common locations for such stealing is the workplace.

Studies show that people justify workplace theft because a corporation doesn't have feelings.[1] People who would never steal

---

1   Dana Wilkie, "Why Is Workplace Theft on the Rise?," SHRM, August 16, 2019, https://www.shrm.org/resourcesandtools/hr-topics/employee-relations/pages/workplace-theft-on-the-rise-.aspx.

money from the wallet of a supervisor will fudge an expense re-
port or steal office supplies without a thought. They steal time by
scrolling social media during work hours or by taking sick leave
when they are not sick. Because the company is less personal, a
crime against it does not feel like an act of violence or contempt.
It feels victimless. And because it is unlikely we will get caught,
we feel safe in our minor trespasses.

Another popular place to secure a five-finger discount is a hotel
room. Hotels routinely lose towels, robes, and even sheets to guests
who would no doubt have taken the lamps if they hadn't been
bolted down. Which is exactly why they are, by the way. Again,
because a hotel doesn't have feelings, we reason no real harm is
done. And because we will be miles away by the time a towel is
discovered to have gone missing, we feel safe in swiping it.

But think how differently we behave when staying in the home
of a friend or relative. Far from stealing the linens, we take care
to make the bed and fold the towel before we depart. The reason
for this change of character has everything to do with the two
critical factors we have noted: relationship and likelihood of
getting caught. We know and are known by the owner. Whereas
a hotel may not notice the loss, our mothers probably would.
And because we care about our mothers, we do not trespass their
property rights.

This is important for Christians to pay attention to. If we
struggle to attribute property rights to a corporation or a hotel
because it is disembodied, how might we struggle to attribute
property rights to an invisible God? And if we mistakenly believe
that an unseen God is also unseeing, how might we be tempted
to trespass all manner of property rights?

No Such Thing as Petty Theft

Indeed, the God who sees our hearts most certainly sees our hands. We are caught red-handed at every turn, whether the boss ever catches us with a stash of staplers or the hotel ever catches us with a trove of towels. Not only does God see us, he knows us. We are known by him. Our behavior with regard to the property of others reveals *how well we know him*. Do we care that he knows us? Or do we regard him as distant and impersonal, disinterested and blind? If we do, we will be prone to taking what is not ours. Ultimately, everything belongs to him. We are guests in his creation, prone to stealing from other guests.

But is it truly necessary to call ourselves out for minor offenses? Yes, make restitution for someone's ox or donkey, but office supplies? Just as the sins of murder and adultery were the end result of a progression of "lesser sins," so also theft starts with small infractions and grows to larger ones (or to a larger number of small infractions). Taking what is not ours shows contempt for the rightful owner. We dare not believe that God does not see or care about these small acts of treachery. For Jesus has told us otherwise:

One who is faithful in a very little is also faithful in much, and one who is dishonest in a very little is also dishonest in much. If then you have not been faithful in the unrighteous wealth, who will entrust to you the true riches? And if you have not been faithful in that which is another's, who will give you that which is your own? (Luke 16:10–12)

Want to be found faithful in much? Begin by being faithful in the little things. To do so will require belief in a relational God who sees. Jacob's theft spoke of his wrong belief that God was disinterested and blind. Arguably, so did that most famous first theft of fruit in the garden. Eve was the first human to learn that the thief comes to kill, steal, and destroy. In her story, he came scaled and slithering, lisping lies. And she, formed to bear the image of God, chose to bear instead the image of the thief. But God was neither disinterested nor blind, nor, thankfully, without pity. For though the thief came to kill, steal, and destroy, Christ was given to put an end to taking. He came to prevent loss, but also to provide abundance (John 10:10). And when we follow his example, we, too, turn our hearts toward providing. The thief takes, the Christ-follower gives.

An Expansive Obedience

The Christ-follower gives as a former thief. We who once heeded the great thief now heed the Spirit of the great giver: "Let the thief no longer steal, but rather let him labor, doing honest work with his own hands, so that he may have something to share with anyone in need" (Eph. 4:28). It is this taker-to-giver transformation which the Westminster Confession acknowledges in its interpretation of the duties required of us by the eighth word: that we would "endeavor, by all just and lawful means, to procure, preserve, and further the wealth and outward estate of others, as well as our own."[2]

---

2 Westminster Larger Catechism, Q. 141; "Larger Catechism: Questions 141–150," Reformed Forum, May 5, 2008, https://reformedforum.org/podcasts/larger-catechism -questions-141-150/.

Let that settle in. We are duty bound to labor for the provision and well-being of others. To borrow the words of Paul, "Let each of you look not only to his own interests, but also to the interests of others" (Phil 2:4). When we understand ourselves to be stewards of God's resources rather than owners, we learn to think differently about earthly treasures. Though the thief whispers that he who has the most toys wins, the giver of all good gifts speaks a better word. Don't just be a *not-thief;* be a provider of abundance.

There are two ways of living: as a taker or as a giver. When it comes to matters of wealth, do you perceive yourself as a terminus or a distribution point? If a terminus, you will labor without rest to acquire that which you cannot keep. If a distribution point, you will labor to give away that which was never truly yours to begin with. When we hear others praying for their daily bread, does it occur to us that we might be the means by which that bread is supplied? The spirit of the eighth word should prompt us to.

I remember once hearing John Bisagno, the great Southern Baptist preacher, admonish the flock regarding giving of their finances to help their neighbors in need. He stood before the congregation and announced jubilantly, "God has all the money he needs to help the needy! It's in your pockets." As providers of abundance, we open our own storehouses to bless others. Instead of a mindset of acquisitiveness, we operate from one of generosity. But not a generosity that is compelled. Rather, we act as former thieves, as those so deeply grateful for the abundance we have received in Christ that we give generously to any who have need.

On Earth as in Heaven

One day thievery will cease. As we saw in our exploration of the first word, the things we long to steal in this life will be the pavestones of the New Jerusalem. Heaven is a place where thieves do not break in. All are at rest in the abundance of God. Jesus tells us that, even while we are still here, we can store up treasure there:

> Fear not, little flock, for it is your Father's good pleasure to give you the kingdom. Sell your possessions, and give to the needy. Provide yourselves with moneybags that do not grow old, with a treasure in the heavens that does not fail, where no thief approaches and no moth destroys. For where your treasure is, there will your heart be also. (Luke 12:32–34)

It is our Father's good pleasure to give the kingdom to all who pray "Thy kingdom come on earth as it is in heaven." When former thieves determine by the power of the Spirit to be faithful in small matters of generosity, they store up treasure in heaven that does not fail. No stock market crash can devalue such treasure. No natural disaster or lawsuit or foreclosure can diminish the value of the generosity expressed by *takers-turned-givers*. When we refrain from taking what is not ours and rush to give what we have received, we make manifest the kingdom here and now.

Stealing is gaining at someone else's unwilling expense. So, Jesus gives us what we could not beg, steal, or borrow, willingly and at great expense. He turns takers into givers by giving what we could never acquire on our own. He restores to us our birthright and blessing, once stolen in a garden by a thief.

It is never too late to turn from our taking. In his final hours of agony, it was a thief whom Jesus forgave. "Today you will be with me in paradise" (Luke 23:43). Friend, while it is still called today, heed the eighth word. Let your hands not grasp for the goods of others. Let your pockets turn loose of their earthly treasures, that all might have daily bread. Your bread is to do the will of him who sent you. He bids you to spread abundance.

Verses for Meditation
Psalm 24:1
Matthew 6:19–21
Luke 16:10–12
John 10:10
Acts 2:44–47
Philippians 2:3–4

Questions for Reflection

1. Before reading this chapter, how would you have rated your obedience to the eighth commandment? After reading it, how would you rate yourself? What new insight accounts for the change in your diagnosis?

2. Think of your earliest memory of stealing. What did you steal? What did you learn as a result? Think of a time someone stole from you. How did you feel about the loss of property? About the thief?

3. What forms of stealing are you most likely to excuse? Why do they seem acceptable? Why are they actually sinful?

4. What act of generosity is the Spirit prompting you toward? What small act of faithfulness might you perform this week with regard to giving of your resources?

Write a prayer asking God to help you to obey the eighth commandment. Confess where you have minimized stealing by believing him to be distant or unseeing. Ask him to help you be a taker-turned-giver, to show you where you might be generous. Praise him that he ordains daily bread to be given to the needy through the ordinary means of our generosity. Thank him for giving you every good gift.

9

The Ninth Word

Honor Reputation

"You shall not bear false witness against your neighbor."
EXODUS 20:16

IN SEASON 5 OF THE COMEDY *Seinfeld*, Jerry, Elaine, Kramer, and George are invited to spend a weekend in the Hamptons. The owner of the home they stay in has just had a baby, who is by all accounts not easy on the eye. Anyone who has seen their share of newborns can sense the perfection of the tension the show creates: What adjectives will we produce when the time arrives for us to express our enthusiasm for the wrinkly little cherub? As Jerry and Elaine shield their eyes and search for kindness, the handsome pediatrician arrives and compliments Elaine as "breathtaking." She is thrilled, but only momentarily, for in his next sentence, he applies the very same word to the baby.

Is the doctor dashing? Yes. Is he trustworthy? Hard to say. The palpable and hilarious doubt introduced by his words illustrates a principle we all tacitly acknowledge: our speech reveals our character. Jesus tells us that there is a direct line from our hearts to our mouths (Matt. 12:34). It is for this reason, and more, that we need the instruction of the ninth word.

As with its three predecessors, the ninth word has to do with taking from our neighbor. We might summarize the sixth through the eighth commands as: don't take your neighbor's life, wife, or stuff. The ninth command will charge us not to take his or her good name. It is appropriate that the ninth word deals with deceptive speech, as no one ever plotted murder, adultery, or theft who did not also commit to lie about it.

In Sunday school as a child, I learned that the ninth word taught "Do not lie." This is true and not true. Lying is addressed in its many forms in the Wisdom Literature of the Bible, but in the ninth word a particular kind of lying is in view: giving false testimony about someone. We might lie about our own actions or credentials or desires, but a lie is distinctly social in nature when it turns its attention to someone else. To lie about someone else directly impacts the health of the community.

Israel's law codes contained many crimes for which the penalty was death, and its justice system relied on the corroborating testimonies of two or three witnesses to establish guilt or innocence. When the ninth word addresses truthfulness about our neighbor, it certainly has legal concerns in view. Lying in a courtroom testimony meant placing the very life of the maligned in jeopardy.

Though the ninth word seeks to ensure that justice function as it should between neighbors, it does not stop there. It can be understood broadly to address the way we speak of and to our neighbors. It commands honesty in our words and actions, a commitment to integrity in rightly representing our neighbors, in both their presence and their absence. Though you may never be called to testify in a court of law, the testimony you bear about your neighbors in everyday moments will shape your life and theirs for good or for ill.

As the third word bade us to honor God's good name, the ninth bids us to honor the good name of our neighbor. Just as we must not misuse the name of the Lord our God, we must not misuse the name of those created in his image. The ninth word builds on the fifth, for it is impossible to honor our elders if we speak falsely about them. The ninth word builds on the sixth, for many who would never contemplate murder commit character assassination without a thought. The ninth word builds on the seventh, for no one enters into adultery without first having lied about the worth of another. The ninth word builds on the eighth, presenting us with an additional angle on thievery, for certainly bearing false witness is identity theft. And the ninth word prepares us to receive the tenth, as we will see in our next chapter.

Giving even the briefest attention to this command, we would likely make a mental note about avoiding some of the more obvious expressions of this sin. But what if we were to truly meditate on this law, looking for an expansive obedience to what it asks? Consider with me these four habits of untruthful (and un-neighborly) speech that, if broken, would bring health to our neighbor and to the community: reviling, flattery, silence, and misattribution.

The Sin of Reviling

We can assume the prevalence of the sin of reviling by the sheer number of times it is addressed in the Bible. Reviling, mocking, and scoffing walk arm in arm through the text, trailed by their brutish cousins, slander and gossip. In the Psalms, reviling revels on the lips of the enemies of God. Proverbs describes the reviler as "one whose rash words are like sword thrusts" (Prov. 12:18). Reviling makes the lists of condemnation in the Epistles, alongside sins like idolatry, theft, drunkenness, and sexual immorality (1 Cor. 5:11; 6:10). Reviling is the contemptuous speech Jesus decries in his discussion of murder, contempt, and anger (Matt. 5:21–26).

While flattery, silence, and misattribution are the subtle pickpockets of reputation, reviling stands in the lobby of First Reputation Bank spraying bullets and sacking the vault. In the modern church, perhaps nothing attests more to our current levels of biblical illiteracy than our casual, thoughtless, and frequent commission of the sin of reviling. See, for example, the virtually indistinguishable difference between our social media use and that of the unbeliever. We routinely exercise our online speech in the business of tearing down the good name of our neighbor the politician, the pastor, or the public figure. The lack of face-to-face interaction increases our boldness, and we become drunk on the adrenaline rush. We are virtual Bonnies and Clydes, with fully loaded keyboards and fully seared consciences.

But social media is just a new vehicle for an old sin, one that works its way into whatever medium it can. We revile with our sarcasm that tears down our neighbor with a wink and a laugh. We revile in correcting our children by shaming through tone and language choice. We revile with our carefully crafted prayer request that smokescreens gossip or slander. We revile in emails and text threads and bumper stickers and casual conversations—in any setting and by any means where we perceive the opportunity to raise our own value by pushing down someone else's.

Who loves reviling? Satan, the father of lies and the accuser of the brethren. When Christians revile, we look and sound like his children. "Out of the same mouth come praise and cursing. My brothers and sisters, this should not be" (James 3:10 NIV). We must refuse to sit in the seat of the scoffer. Jesus Christ refused that unholy throne, and pronounced as blessed those who are reviled for his name: "He committed no sin, neither was deceit found in his mouth. When he was reviled, he did not revile in return" (1 Pet. 2:22–23). Jesus embodies truth, and those who follow him take care to "put away all malice and all deceit and hypocrisy and envy and all slander" (1 Pet. 2:1). Instead, they look for ways to build up others with their speech, and if kind words evade them, they adhere to the basic wisdom of silence.

The Sin of Flattery

When is a compliment not a compliment? When it is offered to cajole or control. Whereas reviling misrepresents by tearing someone down, flattery misrepresents by building someone up. It is manipulation masked as praise, often employed to artificially enhance trust or secure favor. Though we may be tempted to dismiss flattery as relatively harmless, the writer of Proverbs denounces it in strong terms:

> *Whoever hates* disguises himself with his lips
> and harbors deceit in his heart;
> when he speaks graciously, believe him not,
> for there are seven abominations in his heart;

though *his hatred be covered with deception,*

 his wickedness will be exposed in the assembly.

Whoever digs a pit will fall into it,

 and a stone will come back on him who starts it rolling.

A lying tongue hates its victims,

 and a flattering mouth works ruin. (Prov. 26:24–28)

Note the threefold repetition of *hate*. Flattery, like reviling, is hate speech. It is just more subtle in its delivery. Jesus was not taken in or misled by the flattery of those who used it to conceal their hatred toward him. Seeking to trap him, the Pharisees and the Herodians chose honey-coated speech:

> "Teacher, we know that you are true and do not care about anyone's opinion. For you are not swayed by appearances, but truly teach the way of God. Is it lawful to pay taxes to Caesar, or not? Should we pay them, or should we not?" But, knowing their hypocrisy, he said to them, "Why put me to the test?" (Mark 12:14–15)

Taken at face value, their commendation was completely true. But Jesus saw the motive of their hearts. He sees ours, as well. In the words of poet William Blake, "A Truth that's told with bad intent / Beats all the Lies you can invent."[1]

Satan is the father of flattery, delivering it with silver-tongued subtlety. Before he utters a word to Eve, we are told that "the ser-

---

1 William Blake, "Auguries of Innocence," 1863, Poetry Foundation, accessed July 21, 2020, https://www.poetryfoundation.org/poems/43650/auguries-of-innocence.

pent was more subtle than any beast of the field" (Gen 3:1 ASV). And his words bear this out: "You will be like God" (Gen. 3:5). He chooses similar speech when tempting Jesus in the wilderness: "To you I will give all this authority and [worldly] glory" (Luke 4:6). Flattery lures us toward unholy alliances, elevating our sense of self beyond what is justified. When we practice it, we conform to the image of the serpent.

We do well to offer genuine encouragement and praise to one another. Indeed, we are charged to do so (see Prov. 12:25; Eph. 4:29; 1 Thess. 5:11). But our edifying words must be truthful and accurate. Beware those who speak of you in superlatives. No one is served by holding too high an opinion of himself, no matter how well-intended the praise. When we overpraise others, we tempt them into an unholy alliance with pride. Or we tempt them into an unholy alliance with us, that we might manipulate them to our own purposes. We must recognize flattery for what it is: an aggression. As Jon Bloom notes, love never flatters others, and wisdom never desires to be flattered.[2] Praise rightly offered to someone will inspire humility. Truthful praise, offered in genuine encouragement, fulfills the ninth command.

The Sin of Silence

As we have noted, the Bible takes care to commend silence as wisdom. We often neglect holding our tongues when we ought. But Solomon reminds us that there is both "a time to keep silence, and a time to speak" (Eccles. 3:7). When the good name of our

---

2   Jon Bloom, "Lay Aside the Weight of Flattery," Desiring God website, July 21, 2020, https://www.desiringgod.org/articles/lay-aside-the-weight-of-flattery/.

neighbor is run through the mud, the silence of his friends can be as brutalizing as the reviling of his enemies.[3] We must not use the command to be slow to speak as an excuse for never speaking (James 1:19). God help us if we claim to be wise in our silence, when in fact we are masking cowardice.

Sinful silence, like the sin of flattery, is subtle. It may not be immediately clear to those around us whether our silence is properly or wrongly motivated. But it is always clear to God. James reminds us that "whoever knows the right thing to do and fails to do it, for him it is sin" (James 4:17). There are times when we are unsure whether to speak or remain silent. But if we know our words are needed and yet withhold them, we are as guilty of bearing false witness as the reviler who began the lie.

In the early days of his ministry, Jesus would sometimes instruct his followers to remain silent for the time being about who he was. By the time he approached Jerusalem, where he would be crucified, he had already endured much breaking of the ninth word, and much more lay ahead for him. But there, along the road, a multitude of his disciples cried out Hosanna and verbalized the truth of his blessed kingship. When the Pharisees told Jesus to rebuke them, he replied that the time for silence was past: "I tell you, if these were silent, the very stones would cry out" (Luke 19:40).

Who trades in sinful silence? Satan. He likes nothing better than the silence of those who know they should speak. When we silence truth-tellers, or remain silent ourselves when called to

---

3   Spoken in the context of the Civil Rights Movement, Dr. Martin Luther King Jr. captured this idea aptly in his well-known statement: "In the end, we will remember not the words of our enemies, but the silence of our friends."

speak courageously, we conform to Satan's image instead of to the image of Christ. When false witnesses speak against our neighbor, we must speak up to bear true witness on their behalf. Is your impulse to revile? By all means, wisdom begs you to remain silent. Is your impulse to defend the good name of your neighbor? By all means, open your mouth. Courageous speech, given in season, fulfills the ninth command.

gain credit or give blame

The Sin of Misattribution

We saw in our discussion of the third word how we co-opt God's good name to enhance our reputation. In the ninth, we are forbidden from co-opting our neighbor's good name, as well. The sin of misattribution tempts us either to garner credit or shift blame at our neighbor's expense. We bear false witness when we allow our own name to receive glory that belongs to another. If you have ever sat in a meeting and heard your boss take credit for one of your ideas or efforts, you can identify with the need for the ninth word. Garnering credit for someone else's work has never been easier, thanks to the internet and the copy/paste feature. Intellectual property rights recognize the human tendency to break the ninth word. But the practice has always been with us, even when plagiarism was much harder to pull off. Just as we can exalt our own plans by attaching God's name to them, we can exalt our own efforts by concealing the names of others who have labored alongside us or before us. When we commit misattribution, we mask our sloth as genius. Any time we receive praise for work that exceeds the work we performed, we succumb to this sin.

But we also misattribute when we shift blame for sins we ought to own. We glory-hoard when conviction hits. When confronted with our sin, if our first impulse is to say, "_____ made me do it," nimbly filling in the name of our spouse, child, parent, coworker, boss, friend, or enemy, we break the ninth word. We label our neighbor as our excuse, stealing honor by shifting blame, and amplifying our offense in the process. King David's confession to Nathan and to God models the proper attribution of sin: Rather than shout, "Bathsheba made me do it!" he receives Nathan's rebuke of him alone: "*I* have sinned against the LORD" (2 Sam. 12:13; see Ps. 51:1).

Who is a master of misattribution? Satan. He is a practitioner of identity theft, himself masquerading as an angel of light. He celebrates when we steal glory from others, because in doing so, we conform to his image. He delights when we shift blame because it marks us as his disciples. The antidote to misattributed glory-garnering or glory-hoarding is to outdo one another in showing honor. Rather than rushing to take the credit, we must be quick to acknowledge and celebrate the contributions of others. Rather than shifting blame, we must be quick to own sin that is ours alone to own. We must make full and frequent confession without qualifications.

On Earth as in Heaven

In the new heavens and the new earth, there will be an end to the bearing of false witness against our neighbor, made in God's image. Imagine that for a minute. If you have ever felt the sting of being maligned or the shame of having maligned someone, imagine a place where that never, ever happens. If you have ever felt the justness of being rightly represented or the satisfaction of having edified another with your speech, imagine a place where that always and everywhere is the case. Every time we refuse to revile, flatter, go mute, or misappropriate, we live in that future reality today. Every time we choose to speak truthful words, encouraging words, life-giving words, about and to our neighbor, we invite heaven down to earth.

And we make it visible in the here and now. Lying about others comes easiest to us when we believe we can get away with it. The more skilled we grow in bearing false witness, the more frequently we will employ the skill. Like murder, adultery, and theft, we weigh the risk of getting caught and proceed accordingly. The children of God bear in mind that God reads the tell of every human, no matter how impassable the poker face. In speaking of the last days, Jesus warned: "I tell you, on the day of judgment people will give account for every careless word they speak, for by your words you will be justified, and by your words you will be condemned" (Matt. 12:36–37).

We will give an account for every word. Like the ninth word, Jesus's warning is uttered in courtroom language. If we neglect to bear true witness as the ninth word commands, our words will bear witness against us in the day of reckoning.

It is here that I think wistfully of Pinocchio with his wooden nose sprouting branches and leaves. Had God created us to bear a visible sign each time we lied, perhaps we would hesitate as we should. Perhaps if God had been more like Geppetto, we would all employ truth with greater diligence. But God knows better than Geppetto. Nothing bears greater witness to the truth of our invisible God than our visible obedience to his commands. Blessed are those who have not seen and yet obey (John 20:29). Our actions are the incarnation of our belief.

So put away all malice and all deceit and hypocrisy and envy and all slander (1 Pet. 2:1). Put on then, as God's chosen ones, holy and beloved, compassionate hearts, kindness, humility, meekness, and patience. With such a heavenly raiment, who on earth could transgress the ninth word? Let God's kingdom come in the words we choose to bear witness about one another, for so is fulfilled the law of love.

Verses for Meditation
Psalm 1:1–2
Proverbs 12:25
Proverbs 26:24–28
Matthew 12:36–37
James 3:8–12
1 Peter 2:22–23

Questions for Reflection
1. Before reading this chapter, how would you have rated your obedience to the ninth commandment? After reading it, how would you rate yourself? What insight accounts for the change in your diagnosis?

2. How has your understanding of bearing false witness expanded? What deeper obedience have you discovered?

3. Which of the sins of misuse of your neighbor's name are you most prone to commit (reviling, flattery, silence, misattribution)? What heart issue might be driving that pattern of misuse?

4. What situations are most likely to trigger you to misuse the name of your neighbor? Which "neighbor" is usually your tar-

get? How could you change your typical response, both your heart response and your verbal response?

Write a prayer asking God to help you to obey the ninth commandment. Confess where you have fallen short by using your words to defame or diminish the name of your neighbor. Ask him to help you speak of and to your neighbor with truthfulness. Praise him that he does not return our reviling with reviling, but with forgiveness. Thank him for calling you to put away unrighteous speech.

I Peter
2:1

10

The Tenth Word

Honor in the Heart

*"You shall not covet your neighbor's house; you
shall not covet your neighbor's wife, or his male
servant, or his female servant, or his ox, or his
donkey, or anything that is your neighbor's."*

EXODUS 20:17

I ONCE HEARD A PASTOR SAY that we are the belated announcement of what we have been thinking about for the past thirty days.
I have never forgotten it. I can see now that his words rang true
because they were a paraphrase of the tenth word.

In a list of clear prohibitions, the tenth word is unexpected.
For all the other nine, our neighbor could hold us to account
fairly simply by gathering witnesses to testify to our compliance
or lack thereof. But here, at the end of the list, we find a sin of
a different nature. Idol-making, Sabbath-breaking, dishonoring
authority, murder, theft, adultery, and slander can all be identified

by an onlooker, but not so covetousness. Covetousness hides in the heart. The Ten Words progress from "Don't do it" to "Don't say it" to "Don't even think about it."

Jesus has drawn for us a connection to the underlying sin of contempt in his teachings in the Sermon on the Mount. And here, the tenth word acknowledges the truth of his teaching, for no one ever set out to sin against God or neighbor without first desiring something out of bounds. Covetousness and contempt hold hands, for no one ever sought to take from God or neighbor without first desiring to diminish them. Covetousness is a personal offense.

We have seen it in the story of Adam and Eve, who covet what is God's alone. We have seen it in the subsequent story of Cain, who covets what is his brother's. In both of those stories, no human witnesses could be raised to testify to the sins of desire that preceded the sins of action. But there was one who bore witness. The God who sees bears witness to every sinful desire. The tenth word reminds us at the conclusion of what we understood at the outset: there are no gods before God. It is God who bears witness to our compliance to the tenth word. Long before our covetous desires take the visible shape of words or deeds, Yahweh bears witness against us.

If we were to remember this, more readily confessing our sin at the point of desire, perhaps the words of James would not prove so prophetic in our lives: "But each person is tempted when he is lured and enticed by his own desire. Then desire when it has conceived gives birth to sin, and sin when it is fully grown brings forth death" (James 1:14–15).

Desire is a living thing, conceived in the secret place and seeking to grow to maturity. Our words and actions are the birth cry of our mature desires. They are the belated announcement of what we have been thinking about for the past week, month, decade—an unholy and gruesome birth, gestated in our hearts, a confession of a crooked course we committed to some time ago. The tenth word is warning us about promiscuity of thought, and of the heart as a fertile womb.

The grammarian in me does not love a mixed metaphor, but when it emerges from the biblical text, I put to death the grammarian in me. The heart is a place where sin gestates. He who has ears to hear, let him hear.

The tenth word is also unexpected because, like the Sabbath command and the stealing command, it anticipates wealth before Israel has it. The itemizing of house, spouse, servants, and animals paints a portrait of wealth. Only a wealthy neighbor would have such an inventory of covet-worthy status symbols. A nation of recently freed slaves has little to covet. In the earliest years of their freedom, there would have been little stratification of wealth or situation.

Yet God prepares them in advance for the social and emotional complexities that would come their way as wealth increased among the children of God. Just as he decreed rest before any might be tempted to profit off the constant labor of another, God forbids coveting before any might have reason to do so. What a mercy that God sees the end from the beginning. He engraves good boundaries for us even before we know we need them.

For certainly we need the tenth word, today as much as then. Stated in the positive, "Do not covet" becomes "Be content." Covetousness hurts the community because it keeps close company with stinginess. The less content we are with our own possessions, relationships, or circumstances, the less inclined we will be toward the generosity that helps the community flourish. It is contentment we see thriving in the early church in Acts, where everything was shared as any had need (Acts 2:42–47). We do not share with a neighbor when we perceive our own needs to be paramount. Covetousness whispers that we deserve that which has been given to our neighbor. Contentment states plainly that God has given what is good.

Once we connect contentment to covetousness, we can take steps to combat our ungodly desire for the good others have been given. It turns out that contentment is not something that drops from the heavens like manna. It turns out that the route to contentment is open to us if we look for it. Paul gives us the spectacles to see it, in one of the most familiar passages in the New Testament:

> I rejoiced in the Lord greatly that now at length you have revived your concern for me. You were indeed concerned for me, but you had no opportunity. Not that I am speaking of being in need, *for I have learned* in whatever situation I am to be content. I know how to be brought low, and I know how to abound. In any and every circumstance, *I have learned* the secret of facing plenty and hunger, abundance and need. I can do all things through him who strengthens me. (Phil. 4:10–13)

If contentment has been a losing battle for you, if coveting comfort or cash or companions has been your common state, let the good news sink in: *contentment is learned.* It is learned according to the typical pattern of sanctification: through experience, by the power of him who strengthens us. Paul assures us it can be done, and done beyond the bare minimum. He says we can learn contentment *in all things*. But where do we start? If we determine to learn contentment and unlearn coveting, we must start by becoming good students of what fuels our desires.

Note how the progression from house to people to status symbols and "anything that belongs to your neighbor" instructs us in three key areas of coveting: *stuff, relationships, circumstances*. Coveting what someone else has is always a function of a wrong expectation. It is predicated on the idea that we deserve what others have. It feeds on comparison, that old thief of joy, which explains why the covetous person leads a joyless existence of dissatisfaction and contempt. We compare our own situation to that of someone else and allow our expectation to take shape accordingly. The gap between our expectation and our reality is where discontentment and covetousness thrive. As long as our expectations exceed our current reality, we will be particularly prone to break the tenth word.

It is not wrong to have expectations for our stuff, our relationships, and our circumstances—it is just wrong to have *unrealistic* expectations. As the tenth word points out, we are deeply concerned with keeping up with the Joneses. We want to have a kitchen like their kitchen, a marriage like their marriage, vacations and cars like theirs, smart and athletic children like theirs, flexible work arrangements like theirs. Whatever they've got, we would like—only slightly better, as long as we're making an adjustment to the balance sheets.

Why do we want it? We illustrate the wisdom of the French proverb: "What makes us discontented with our condition is the absurdly exaggerated idea we have of the happiness of others." When we look at our neighbor and covet his stuff, relationships, or circumstances, we commit the grave error of assuming that his stuff, relationships, or circumstances have made him happier than we are. We are actually ridiculous enough to think that if we had what he had, we would be happy.

The Bible provides us a lengthy cautionary tale about comparison to our neighbor. We might title it "Keeping Up with the Canaanites." It shows us that Israel as a whole soon forgot the tenth word in a rush to compare with her neighbors. In a scene that reads like a middle schooler asking for the latest pair of shoes, Israel asks God to give her a king like the other nations.[1] God decides to teach his people contentment the hard way, by giving them what they want. Saul's disastrous reign is the result.

The Pull of the Past

What led Israel to want such a king? Like us, the expectation was formed not just by her present, but in large part by her past. We want what we had, or what we never had. In Israel's case, the sting of slavery to the Pharaohs would have heightened their desire to have their own majestic ruler as the ultimate proof that they were slaves no more. Their Egypt experience was one they simultaneously loathed and longed to return to. Every time their bellies rumbled, they looked over their shoulders with longing. Like Israel, the way we view our present is shaped by the way we view our past.

Our expectation for what neighborhood we should live in is a product of the one we grew up in. Our expectation for our spouse is shaped by the marriage we witnessed in our home of origin. Our

---

1   The story of Israel asking for Saul as king can be found in 1 Samuel 8 and the following chapters.

expectation for our body shape is tied to the way we used to look. We are formed by our formative years, either positively or negatively. We want to be just like our parents, or we want to be nothing like them. We want the abs and smooth skin of our twenties, or we want to be leaner or stronger than our adolescent selves. We want our husband to be just like our father or nothing like him at all. Our past experience dictates the way we inhabit the present, the desires we feed or starve, and the habits we build or break.

Whether we view the past as a place that was better or as a place we want to forget, our expectations for the present reflect the experiences we have lived. If an expectation shaped by your past is causing you to covet in the present, perhaps it's time to become a student of those expectations and desires. Rose-colored glasses are as dangerous as regret when it comes to leveraging the past to shape the present. The more prone we are to wanting now to be like then, or completely unlike then, the more likely we are to ask our stuff, our relationships, or our circumstances to meet an expectation they simply can't. Instead, we can trust the past to the God of yesterday, and ask him to help us see today clearly.

The Idolatry of an Ideal

Just as our past can shape our expectations and warp our contentment, so also can comparisons to an ideal. The world presents us with its version of the good life at every turn, through any medium with the power to influence the masses. Advertisements sell us an idea of ourselves as successful, attractive, or powerful. Movies and TV shows define ideal relationships, selling us versions of romance, friendship, and family that are either unattainable or ungodly. Even our own friends are selling a version of the good life via their curated social media accounts: tablescapes, vacations, and dieting successes all handpicked for the flattering lens they offer.

Who among us has not watched a romantic comedy and compared our own romance? Who among us has not watched a home makeover show and not wanted to burn our own house to the ground? When battling expectations set by an ideal, it is good to remember exactly what an ideal is. *Webster's* dictionary defines *ideal* as "existing as a mental image or in fancy or imagination only."[2] The ideal job, spouse, family, home, or paycheck that is being dangled before us by media outlets is—let's say it together—*not real*. It is detached from reality, false, a mortal enemy of contentment and a bosom buddy of covetousness.

How can we battle the false expectations raised by an ideal? One key skill on the road to learning contentment is to limit our exposure to desire-enhancing sources. As we noted in our discussion of the seventh word, it hurts to look. Maybe turn off HGTV. Maybe pitch those catalogs in the recycle bin unread. Maybe stop scrolling social media. If your rom-com causes you to sin, cut it off. You get the idea. Go forth and conquer.

Jesus and Comparison

Jesus warned, "Take care, and be on your guard against all covetousness, for one's life does not consist in the abundance of his possessions" (Luke 12:15). To live a life that consists in the abundance of possessions is inconsistent with abundant life.

Perhaps the most sinister aspect of covetousness is the way that it keeps our eyes fixed on the horizontal plane. When we reject the

2 *Merriam-Webster*, s.v. "ideal," accessed October 12, 2020, www.merriam-webster.com /dictionary/ideal.

tenth word, we say, in effect, "I will cast down my eyes unto the dirt. From whence cometh my help? My help cometh from the world."[3] Rather than desire the well-being of my neighbor, I desire his stuff, relationships, and circumstances. It is impossible to want the best for another while wanting these things. The great loss of a covetous life is that it keeps love of self as our primary concern. If we love the Great Commandment, we must love the tenth word.

Jesus did not love the world or anything in it, renouncing the worldliness that the tenth word addresses. The love of the Father was in him, and his desires were turned wholly toward securing the good of his neighbor. His eyes were not fixed on the horizontal plane, but on the vertical—to the holy hill of God from whence his help, and ours, would surely come.

Yes, evil desire, when it has conceived, gives birth to sin, and sin, when it is fully grown, brings forth death. But his was holy desire. Holy desire, when it has conceived, gives birth to righteousness, and righteousness, when it is fully grown, brings forth life. This righteousness is birthed in all who are joined to Christ in faith. Thus, we learn to love the tenth word, praying, *Lead us in the path of righteousness for thy name's sake.*[4]

On Earth as in Heaven

What is more exhausting than covetousness? What is more wearying than comparing to confirm a suspicion that someone else has it better than we do? What is more like Satan than to want what belongs to another?

3   See Ps. 121:1–2.
4   Ps. 23:3

In the new heavens and earth, we will cease our coveting. We will not be tied to comparison, at last gazing unhindered on the one without compare. We will have obtained fully the pearl of great price. We will have unearthed completely the treasure hidden in a field. We will be free of the suspicion that someone else has it better than we do. We will know beyond a doubt that the greatest possession, the purest relationship, the highest circumstance is ours for eternity. We will enjoy in full the great gain of godliness with contentment.[5]

But godliness with contentment is great gain here and now. Why wait until then to live as a citizen of the kingdom of heaven? When we reject covetousness and embrace the tenth word, we pray "Thy kingdom come." We fix our eyes heavenward, and we open our hearts to seek the well-being of our neighbor, free from envy. What is more like Christ than to want the good of our neighbor? What better way to spend this life than in the laying down of pointless comparison and the taking up of comparison to Christ? This is the here-and-now abundant life offered to us through the words of the tenth commandment, the life that holy desire alone can bring forth. We are the belated announcement of what we have been thinking about the past thirty days. Beloved, always and everywhere, think on these things.

Verses for Meditation
Luke 12:15
Ephesians 5:1–3

want good for others

5   1 Tim. 6:6

1 Timothy 6:6–9
James 1:13–15

Questions for Reflection

1. Before reading this chapter, how would you have rated your obedience to the tenth commandment? After reading it, how would you rate yourself? What insight accounts for the change in your diagnosis?

2. How has your understanding of covetousness and contentment expanded?

3. Which of the comparison points holds the strongest grip on your expectations (others, the past, an ideal)? What steps might you take to learn contentment by limiting comparison?

4. What are you most likely to covet: stuff, relationships, or circumstances? What person is most likely to be the object of your envy? Commit to pray for that person's well-being and blessing this week.

Write a prayer asking God to help you to obey the tenth commandment. Confess where you have fallen short by coveting what is not yours. Ask him to help you learn contentment in place of covetousness. Praise him that he is the giver of all good gifts. Thank him for giving Christ as the pattern for self-forgetfulness.

Conclusion

Delight to Remember

*". . . but his delight is in the law of the LORD,
and on his law he meditates day and night."*

PSALM 1:2

TEN WORDS TO LIVE BY. Ten Words to show us the pattern of Christlikeness and to stir in us a longing for the kingdom to come. Ten Words to convict us, to shape us, and to give us hope. Ten Words that Jesus came not to abolish, but to fulfill.

Though for us they are prohibitions, for Jesus they proved prophetic. The Ten Words rest like a benediction from the Father to the Son on the eve of the incarnation:

You shall have no gods before me.

You shall not make a graven image.

You shall not take my name in vain or break my Sabbath.

You shall honor earthly authority.

You shall not murder, or commit adultery, or steal, or bear false witness.

You shall not covet the estate of another.

Jesus Christ delighted to fulfill the law, opening the gate of salvation. "And there is salvation in no one else, for there is no other name under heaven given among men by which we must be saved" (Acts 4:12).

The law will be either our demise or our delight. Jesus speaks in the Sermon on the Mount of a broad path that leads to destruction and a narrow path that leads to life (Matt. 7:14). The broad path is wide to accommodate everyone from the legalist to the libertine. Whether you choose an outward show of moralism or you chuck the law completely, there is room for you here. The narrow path is narrow because its gate is Christ alone, and its way is the way of holiness. It is the path that teaches us the delight of loving God and neighbor as we look toward a day when all will be made new.

The narrow path is the closest place to heaven on earth we can know in this life.

Do we stumble along the way? Yes. Though ransomed and redeemed, we still falter, relearning again the gift of grace. But we cannot be taken from the narrow path. Its destination is sure. And the longer we walk it, the more we grow to look like the one who walked it first and best, the one of whom it is said, "I delight to do your will, O my God; / your law is within my heart" (Ps. 40:8).

In Christ is sealed the covenant spoken of by the prophet Jeremiah:

> For this is the covenant that I will make with the house of Israel after those days, declares the LORD: I will put my law within them, and I will write it on their hearts. And I will be their God, and they shall be my people. (Jer. 31:33)

No more external obedience. Obedience that pleases God begins in the heart. Ten Words carved in stone at Sinai and powerless to save us, now carved on our hearts and powerful to transform us. The tablets given to Moses have long since crumbled to dust, but the beauty of their commands lives on from generation to generation in the hearts of God's people. It singles us out as strangers in a strange land. We are nomads still, citizens of another place, passing through this present wilderness filled with longing for permanence, for a city that has foundations, whose designer and builder is God.[1]

Ten Words to put to death our sin. Ten Words to herald abundant life. Ten Words to steady and strengthen us on the narrow path that leads us home. In the New Jerusalem, the gates of our homecoming will never be closed. One day, we will enter those gates with thanksgiving. May it be said of us on that day that our meditative delight was in the law of the Lord. May it be said of us that in thought, word, and deed, we remembered to delight.

1   Heb. 11:10

General Index

Scripture Index

Also Available from Jen Wilkin

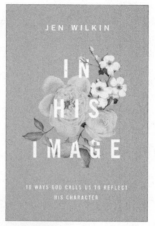

Personal Reflections

Personal Reflections

Personal Reflections

Personal Reflections

Personal Reflections